Science

Reading Support and Homework

Grade 4

Orlando Austin New York San Diego Toronto London

Visit *The Learning Site!*
www.harcourtschool.com

Printed in the United States of America

ISBN 0-15-343606-9

10 11 12 13 14 15 16 1421 15 14 13 12 11 10 09

Contents

Chapter 4 Understanding Ecosystems

Chapter 5 Energy Transfer in Ecosystems

Chapter 6 The Rock Cycle

Chapter 7 Changes to Earth's Surface

Chapter 8 The Water Cycle

Chapter 9 Planets and Other Objects in Space

Chapter 14 Making and Using Electricity

Chapter 15 Forces and Motion

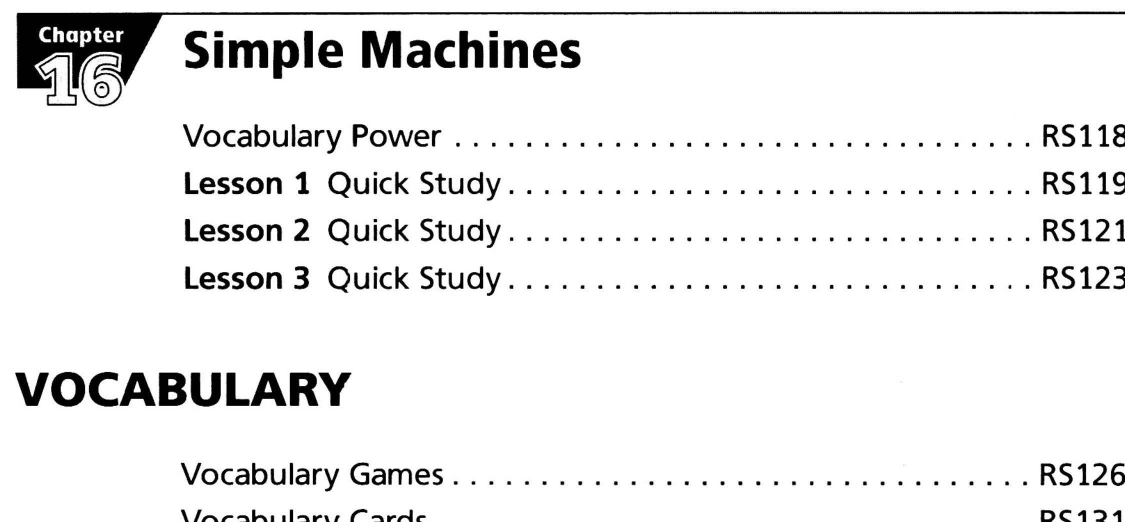

Chapter 16 Simple Machines

VOCABULARY

Name ______________________

Date ______________________

Getting to Know Your Textbook

Welcome to *Science* by Harcourt School Publishers. You can look forward to an exciting year of discovery.

Your textbook has many features that can help you learn science this year. Use this scavenger hunt to learn more about it.

1. What animal is on the cover of your book? ______________________

Name one fact about the animal. ______________________

2. What is the copyright year of your book? ______________________

3. How many authors are there? Name one. ______________________

____

4. How many chapters are in your book? Name one. ______________________

____

5. Find the chapter called "Getting Ready for Science." Name one of the science tools you will use this year. ______________________

6. Name two of the steps of the Scientific Method, found in the same chapter.

____

____

7. What are the three handbooks in the back of your book? ______________________

____

8. What Reading Focus Skill is used in Lesson 1 of Chapter 2?

____

9. What is the first word in the glossary? ______________________

10. What is the last term listed in the index? ______________________

Name ______________________________

11. Name the title and page number of an Investigate you would like to try.

____

12. Name the title and page number of an Insta-Lab you would like to try.

____

13. Name the title and page number of a Science Project for Home or School you would like to try. ____

14. What three types of links are found at the end of Lesson 2 in Chapter 3?

____

15. Find a Fast Fact that you find interesting. Write its title and page number.

____

16. What is the title of the Science Up Close feature in Chapter 5?

____

17. Turn to page R36. What is one way you can be safe when doing experiments?

____

18. The Science Spin features come from what magazine?

____

19. Write the name of a person featured in one of the Science Spin People features. ____

20. Write three new things you expect to learn about this year.

____

____

Name ______________________________

Date ______________________________

Compare and Contrast Animals

Informative Writing–Compare and Contrast

Write a paragraph that will help a younger child tell the difference between a worm and a snail. Tell how these two animals are alike and how they are different. Use the Venn diagram below to help you organize your writing.

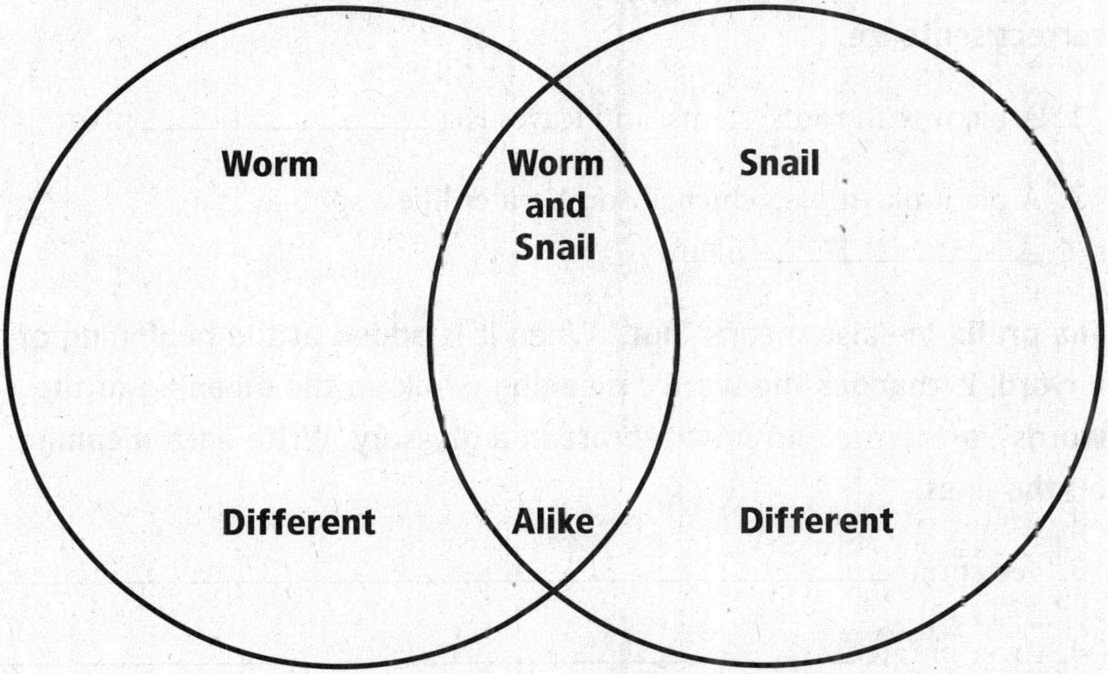

Worm	Worm and Snail	Snail
Different	Alike	Different

____

____

____

____

____

____

____

____

____

Name ______________________________

Date ______________________________

Vocabulary Power

Classifying Living Things

A. Prefixes *in–*, *non–*

The prefix *non–* means "not." When it is added at the beginning of a word, it changes the word's meaning. Look up the words *vascular* and *nonvascular* in a glossary. Then write the correct word in the correct sentence.

1. A plant with roots, stems, and leaves is a ______________ plant.

2. A plant like moss, which absorbs water like a sponge, is a ______________ plant.

The prefix *in–* also means "not." When it is added at the beginning of a word, it changes the word's meaning. Look up the meaning of the words *vertebrate* and *invertebrate* in a glossary. Write each meaning on the lines.

3. vertebrate ____

4. invertebrate ____

Write *vertebrate* or *invertebrate* next to each animal's name to classify the animal.

5. gorilla ______________

6. rattlesnake ______________

7. jellyfish ______________

8. frog ______________

9. hummingbird ______________

10. slug ______________

Name ______________________________

Date ______________________________

Lesson Quick Study

Lesson 1 - How Are Living Things Classified?

1. **Inquiry Skill Practice–Use Models**

How would you use a balloon to model bacteria? Explain your reasoning.

____

____

2. **Use Vocabulary**

Match the clue on the left to the term on the right.

____ A one-celled organism with a nucleus

____ A living thing

____ Something that cannot be seen with the eyes alone

____ A one-celled organism without a nucleus

A. organism

B. microscopic

C. bacteria

D. protist

3. Focus Skill **Reading Skill Practice–Main Idea and Details**

Read the selection. Underline the main idea. List at least 3 details about the main idea.

Bacteria are the most abundant organisms on Earth. They are probably the oldest too. Bacteria are grouped by their shapes. Some bacteria are rod-shaped. Some other bacteria are shaped like balls. Still other bacteria are spiral-shaped. But does that mean that all bacteria in the same group are identical? No! The shape of the bacteria can vary when seen through a microscope. For example, some rod-shaped bacteria can be shorter, longer, thinner, or thicker, yet remain rod-shaped bacteria.

____

Name ________________________________

4. Focus Skill **Main Idea and Details**

Use this space to complete the graphic organizer shown in the Reading Review of the Student Edition.

Copy and complete this chart.

Kingdom	Food Source	Movement	Cell Traits
Animals	A ____________	move around	have a nucleus
Plants	make food	B ____________	have a cell C ____________
Protists	D ____________	most move about	one-celled organisms
Fungi	can't make own food	E ____________	have a cell wall
Bacteria	some make food, some don't	some move about	F ____________

5. **Critical Thinking and Problem Solving**

Suppose you are looking through a microscope. You are told that what you are looking at is a cell. You are asked to identify the cell as a plant cell or an animal cell. How would you be able to tell the difference? Explain.

____

____

____

____

____

Name ______________________________

Date ______________________________

Lesson 2 - How Are Plants and Fungi Classified?

1. Inquiry Skill Practice–Use Space Relationships

You know that nonvascular plants absorb water and nutrients like a sponge. But vascular plants have a system in place to deliver water and nutrients to the parts of the plant. Describe how water and nutrients move through vascular plants.

____

2. Use Vocabulary

Complete each sentence with the correct term from the box.

vascular
nonvascular
fungi

______________ plants are those that do not have channels that carry food and water throughout the plant.

Organisms that absorb food and can't move about are referred to as ______________.

______________ plants are those that have channels that carry food and water throughout the plant.

3. Focus Skill Reading Skill Practice–Main Idea and Details

Read the selection. Underline the main idea. List at least 3 details.

Fungi look like plants. Fungi were once considered part of the plant kingdom. Plants and fungi are different in one important way. Fungi lack chloroplasts; therefore, they cannot make their own food. Fungi absorb nutrients from plants and their decaying materials. They break down the nutrients, absorbing them into their cells.

____

____

Name ______________________________

4. Focus Skill **Main Idea and Details**

Use this space to complete the graphic organizer shown in the Reading Review of the Student Edition.

Copy and complete this graphic organizer.

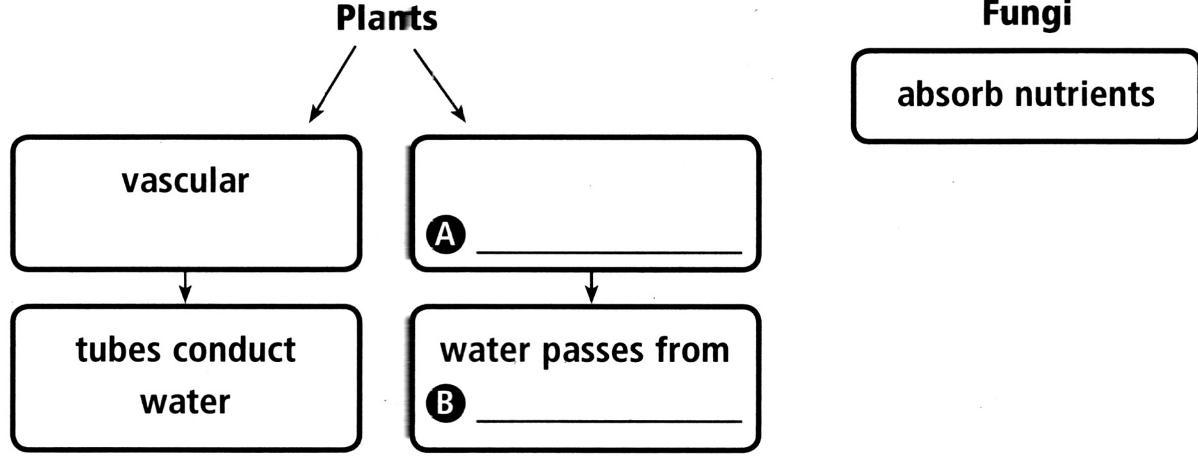

5. **Critical Thinking and Problem Solving**

How is a vascular plant similar to a person drinking water through a straw? Explain your reasoning.

____

____

____

____

____

____

Name ______________________________
Date ______________________________

Lesson 3 - How Are Animals Classified?

1. Inquiry Skill Practice–Plan a Simple Investigation

You know that vertebrates have a backbone to support their body structure. But now you are curious if the size of a backbone determines how big an animal can get. Plan a simple experiment to find out.

____

2. Use Vocabulary

Write a complete sentence that uses the term correctly.

vertebrates: ____

invertebrates: ____

3. Focus Skill Reading Skill Practice–Main Idea and Details

Read the selection. Underline the main idea. List at least 3 details.

Invertebrates are those animals that do not have a backbone. Arthropods are invertebrates. They do not have a backbone. Arthropods can be found almost everywhere on Earth. Some arthropods include spiders and shrimps. Arthropods have jointed legs. They have an exoskeleton, or rigid skin covering the outside of their body. When the arthropods grow, they shed the old exoskeleton and grow a new one.

____

____

____

Name ______________________________

4. Main Idea and Details

Use this space to complete the graphic organizer shown in the Reading Review of the Student Edition.

Copy this chart and fill in the boxes.

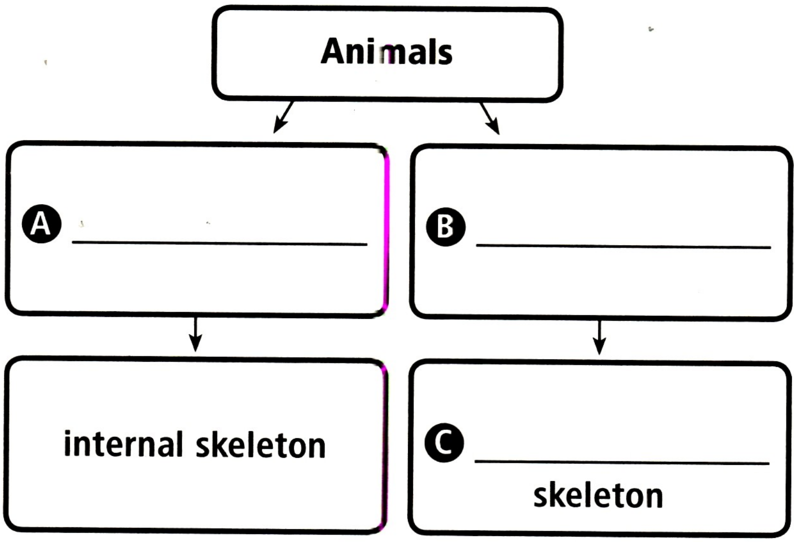

5. Critical Thinking and Problem Solving

We are vertebrates. We have a backbone. Our backbone is what supports our bones in our body. Imagine that you could take your backbone out of your body without causing any damage. What do you think will happen? Explain.

____

____

____

____

____

Name ______________________
Date ______________________

Vocabulary Power

Life Cycles

A. Context Clues

Read the words in the Word Box and look them up in a glossary. Then complete the sentences below. Use the sentence context to help you choose the correct term for each sentence.

direct development	heredity	trait

1. Among other characteristics, the girl inherited the ______________ for curly red hair from her uncle on her mother's side.

2. The male and female poodles passed their black coat color to their offspring through ______________.

3. In the process known as ______________, living things like baby spiders look like smaller versions of their parents.

B. Related Words

Write the term from the box that you believe is related to each group of words.

gene	life cycle
heredity	metamorphosis

4. inheritance **heritage** **heir** ______________	**6. metabolism** **mesomorph** **Morpheus** ______________
5. geneticist **gene pool** **genealogy** ______________	**7. rock cycle** **water cycle** **recycle** ______________

Name ______________________

Date ______________________

Lesson Quick Study

Lesson 1 - What Is Heredity?

1. Inquiry Skill Practice–Conclude Based on Observations

Look at the chart to the right. What conclusions can you make about the eye color of these families?

Parents/Eye Color	Children
Mother: blue Father: blue	Child 1: blue Child 2: blue
Mother: brown Father: brown	Child 1: brown Child 2: brown
Mother: brown Father: blue	Child 1 brown Child 2 brown

____

____

____

____

2. Use Vocabulary

Complete each sentence with the correct term from the box.

trait heredity gene

______________ is when traits are passed from parents to offspring.

______________ are what carry the instructions for how organisms will grow and develop.

A characteristic that makes an organism different is a ______________.

3. Focus Skill Reading Skill Practice–Main Idea and Details

Read the selection. Underline the main idea. Circle at least 2 details about the main idea.

Is your hair like your mom's or your dad's? You inherit traits from your parents that determine the way your hair would look. But what if your dad has short hair and yours is long? What if your mom dyes her hair black and yours is blonde? Cutting your hair or having it long, as well as dying it, are choices we make. The traits we inherit are unique.

Name ______________________________

4. Focus Skill **Main Idea and Details**

Use this space to complete the graphic organizer shown in the Reading Review of the Student Edition.

Copy and complete the graphic organizer.

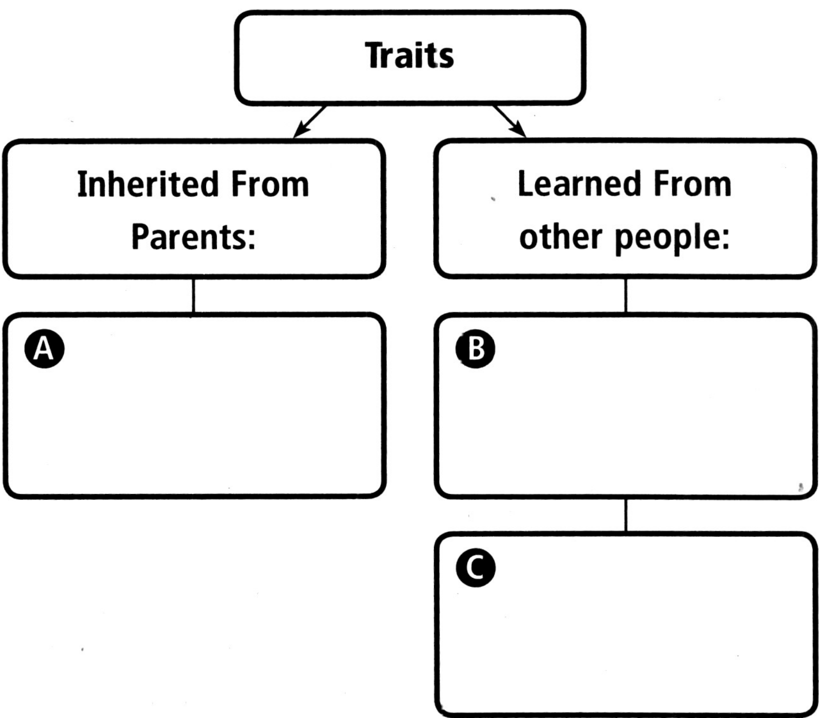

5. **Critical Thinking and Problem Solving**

Imagine you are a reptile that just hatched from an egg. You look around in search for your parents but see nothing. You search for others of your kind. Now you must learn certain traits that will help you survive. What are those possible traits you need to learn from others around you?

____

____

____

Name ______________________________
Date ______________________________

Lesson 2 - What Are Some Life Cycles of Plants?

1. Inquiry Skill Practice–Hypothesize

Rita put a bean seed in a cup with moist cotton. She labeled it ***Seed A***. She then put another bean seed in a cup with dirt. She labeled it ***Seed B***. She placed the cup labeled ***Seed A*** near a window. She placed the cup labeled ***Seed B*** in her drawer. Hypothesize what will happen to each seed. Explain.

____

____

____

____

2. Use Vocabulary

Write a complete sentence that uses the words *life cycle* correctly.

____

3. Focus Skill Reading Skill Practice–Sequence

Put the following events about the plant life cycle in the correct sequence. Number the steps 1 to 5.

____ The new plant, or seedling, grows leaves and makes its own food.

____ Animals eat the fruits and drop their seeds; with the right conditions, the plant life cycle starts again.

____ The seed swells and cracks open, and the embryo starts to germinate.

____ Pollinated flowers grow into fruits that surround the seeds.

____ Flowers grow and produce pollen.

Name ____________________________

4. Focus Skill **Sequence**

Use this space to complete the graphic organizer shown in the Reading Review of the Student Edition.

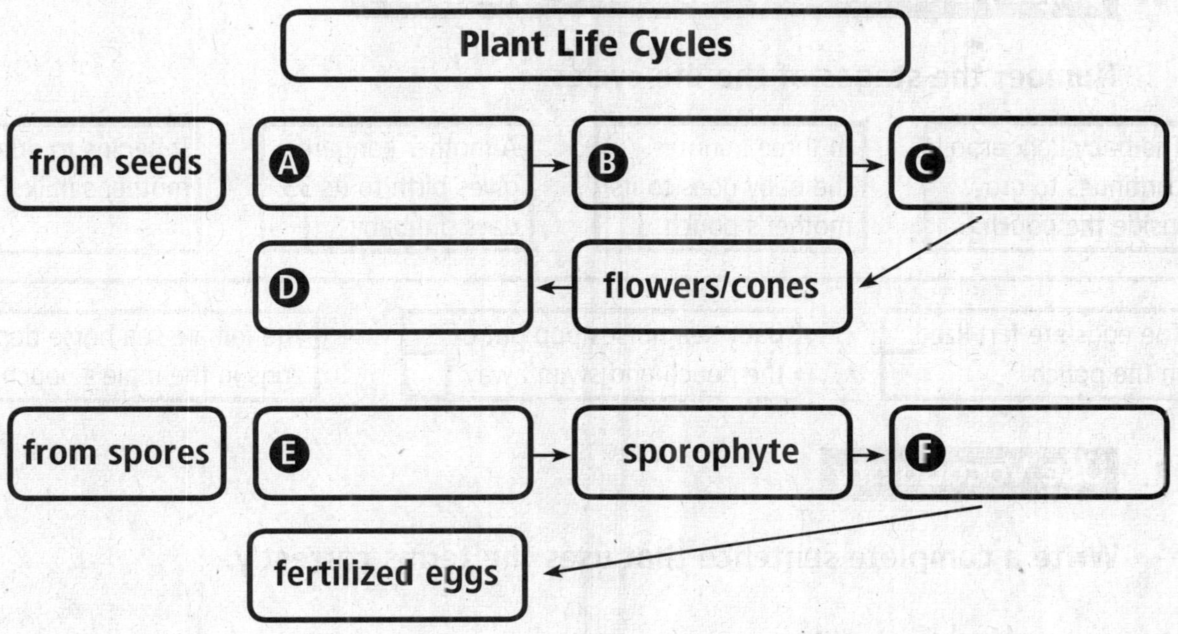

5. **Critical Thinking and Problem Solving**

You learned that a seed is sometimes taken from one place to another. If it lands in a place where the conditions are right for its growth, the seed will develop and grow into a new plant. What are three ways a seed can be taken from one place to another?

____

____

____

____

____

Name ______________________

Date ______________________

Lesson 3 - What Are Some Life Cycles of Animals?

1. Inquiry Skill Practice–Compare and Order

Number the stages of the life cycles.

The baby kangaroo continues to grow inside the pouch. ☐	In three minutes the baby goes to its mother's pouch. ☐	A mother kangaroo gives birth to its 33 days old baby. ☐	It begins to drink its mother's milk. ☐

The eggs are fertilized in the pouch. ☐	Baby sea horses pop out of the pouch and swim away. ☐	The female sea horse deposits eggs in the male's pouch. ☐

2. Use Vocabulary

Write a complete sentence that uses the terms correctly.

direct development ______________________

metamorphosis ______________________

3.  Reading Skill Practice–Compare and Contrast

Read the selection. Compare and contrast the growth rates.

A dog and a frog grow and develop, but their life cycles are not the same. A dog is born from its mother with wobbly legs, baby teeth, and closed eyes. Its face and body will get bigger and longer, but it will look much as it would in its adult life. A tadpole hatches from an egg with a tail and gills. With time, it loses its tail and grows legs. Its lungs develop and the tadpole hops onto land as a frog.

____

____

Name ___________________________

4. Focus Skill **Compare and Contrast**

Use this space to complete the graphic organizer shown in the Reading Review of the Student Edition.

Copy and complete the graphic organizer.

complete metamorphosis	**A four stages:**
direct development	**B**
human life cycle	**C four stages:**

5. **Critical Thinking and Problem Solving**

You learned that when an animal goes through major changes in its life cycle, like a frog, it undergoes metamorphosis. Some other animals, like the grasshopper, go through what is called incomplete metamorphosis. If the grasshopper goes through changes just as the frog does, why do you suppose these changes are referred to as *incomplete* metamorphosis and not metamorphosis? Explain.

____

____

____

____

____

Name ______________________________
Date ______________________________

Adaptations

A. Suffixes

The suffix *–tion* changes a verb into a noun that means "the act of doing something." For example, the verb *conserve* means "to save resources by using them wisely." *Conservation* means "the act of conserving." Add the suffix *–tion* to the words below to form a new word. Then write the definition of the new word.

1. adapt + tion ______________________________

2. hibernate + tion ______________________________

3. extinct + tion ______________________________

4. migrate + tion ______________________________

B. Explore Word Meanings

Now answer these questions. Think about the meaning of the underlined words.

5. Extinction means that all the members of a certain group of organisms have died. Does extinction describe pandas or woolly mammoths?

____

6. An adaptation is a body part or a behavior that helps a living thing survive. Which of these is an example of an adaptation—a lizard's long tongue or a dog's collar?

____

7. Hibernation means "to enter a dormant, inactive state." Which animal hibernates in winter—a zebra or a woodchuck?

____

Name ______________________________

Date ______________________________

Lesson 1 - How Do the Bodies of Animals Help Them Meet Their Needs?

1. **Inquiry Skill Practice–Draw Conclusions**

The basic needs to survive are food, water, air, and shelter. Some animals hibernate during the winter. During this time, they do not eat or drink anything. Conclude how it is that they can survive.

____

____

____

2. **Use Vocabulary**

Write a complete sentence that uses the words *basic needs* correctly.

____

Write a complete sentence that uses the word *adaptation* correctly.

____

3. Focus Skill **Reading Skill Practice–Main Idea and Details**

Read the selection. Underline the main idea. List at least two details about the main idea.

Some birds migrate, or travel during the winter to warmer places to find food, water, and shelter. During the winter, the trees loose their leaves and the birds' shelters become cold and unprotected. It is also difficult for birds to find food. If birds do not migrate during the winter, they will not be able to survive. When temperatures warm up again, the birds return to their original homes.

____

Name ______________________________

4. Focus Skill **Main Idea and Details**

Complete this graphic organizer.

Main Idea: Animals develop adaptations to meet their needs.

An adaptation to meet the need for food: Ⓐ ______________________________

____

An adaptation to meet the need for water: Ⓑ ______________________________

____

An adaptation to meet the need for shelter: Ⓒ ______________________________

____

5. **Critical Thinking and Problem Solving**

How is plant behavior in winter like an animal migrating?

____

____

____

____

____

____

Name ______________________________

Date ______________________________

Lesson 2 - How Do the Behaviors of Animals Help Them Meet Their Needs?

1. Inquiry Skill Practice–Observe

Imagine that two wolves are born from the same mother. One of the wolves is taken to the wild. The other wolf is given to a trainer. What differences in behavior might you observe on the two wolves after a few years have passed?

____

____

2. Use Vocabulary

Match the clue on the left to the term on the right.

____ The state in which animals become dormant.

____ The behaviors that older animals teach younger animals

____ Behaviors animals are born with that help them meet their needs

A. Instinct

B. Hibernation

C. Learned behavior

3. Focus Skill Reading Skill Practice–Main Idea and Details

Read the selection. Underline the main idea. Circle at least three details about the main idea.

Sometimes the instincts that animals are born with are not enough to help them survive. Animals need to learn behaviors from other animals. A bear cub is born knowing how to get milk from its mother. It also knows how to cry if it is hungry. But a bear must teach its cubs to climb trees for safety, hunt for food, and find shelter.

Name ___________________________

4. Focus Skill **Main Idea and Details**

Complete this graphic organizer.

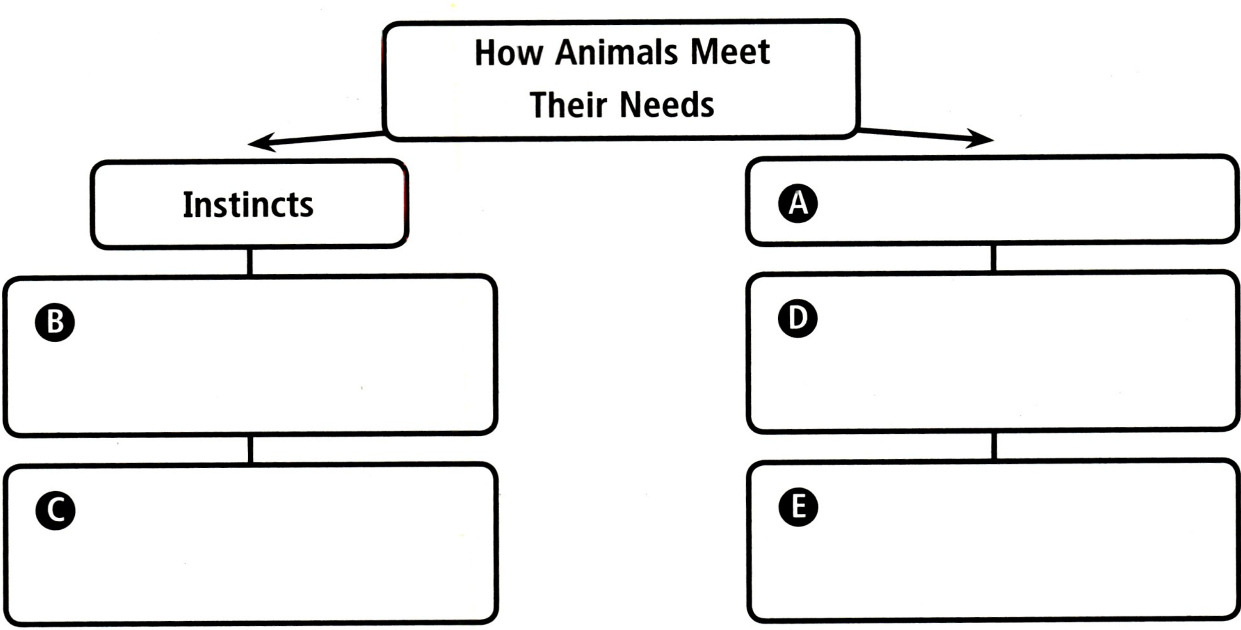

5. **Critical Thinking and Problem Solving**

Many places are very cold during the winter. If an animal does not have adaptations to live through the cold winter, what two things could it do to survive until the spring? Explain.

____

____

____

____

____

Name ______________________________

Date ______________________________

Lesson 3 - How Do Living Things of the Past Compare with Those of Today?

1. **Inquiry Skill Practice–Observe and Infer**

Sandra observed that a rock had a fossil of a leaf on its surface. What can Sandra infer about her observation?

____

____

____

2. **Use Vocabulary**

Complete each sentence with the correct term from the box.

fossil
extinction

The scientist studies the ______________ carefully to identify how this plant from long ago is similar to the ones that live today. ______________ means that many animals from long ago no longer exist.

3. Focus Skill **Reading Skill Practice–Compare and Contrast**

Read the selection. Compare and contrast the different animals.

Fossils often show how animals of long ago were the same or different from animals of today. A fossil of a triceratops shows that its body shape and horned nose are similar to that of the rhinoceros. The triceratops' teeth indicate that this animal ate plants. Rhinoceroses eat grass. Triceratopses were large animals that moved slowly, like the rhinoceroses.

____

____

____

Name ______________________________

4. Focus Skill Compare and Contrast

Complete this graphic organizer.

One way a rhinoceros and a triceratops are the same	One way a rhinoceros and a triceratops are different

5. Critical Thinking and Problem Solving

Imagine you live in a location where a saltwater marsh is being filled in to build a shopping center. A species of bird and a plant are both threatened by their loss of habitat. Which would be more likely to become extinct and why?

____

____

____

____

Name ______________________________

Date ______________________________

Describe an Ecosystem

Informative Writing–Description

Think of a park or other natural area you like to visit. Using the outline below to help you organize, write a paragraph describing this place as an ecosystem. Illustrate your paragraph with a diagram identifying living and nonliving parts of the ecosystem. Label inputs and outputs.

Name of the park or natural area:	Diagram of system:
Living parts of the ecosystem:	
Nonliving parts of the ecosystem:	
Inputs to the ecosystem:	
Outputs from the ecosystem:	

Name ______________________

Date ______________________

Vocabulary Power

Understanding Ecosystems

A. Suffixes

Adding a suffix to a word changes its meaning and usage. The suffixes *–tion*, *–ation*, *–ity*, and *–ment* make nouns out of verbs and adjectives. Add suffixes to each of the following words. Then write what the new word means. Use a glossary to help you, if necessary.

Suffix	Meaning
–ity	state or quality
–ment	something that
–tion, –ation	the act of doing something

1. adapt + ation ______________________
2. commune + ity ______________________
3. diverse + ity ______________________
4. environ + ment ______________________
5. populate + tion ______________________

B. Greek Roots and Prefixes

The words *biotic* and *abiotic* contain the Greek root *–bio,* meaning "life." The prefix *a–* means "not." Choose the words from the box that are examples of the terms.

soil	plants	sunlight
water	air	animals

6. biotic ______________________
7. abiotic ______________________

Name ______________________________

Date ______________________________

Lesson 1 - What Are the Parts of an Ecosystem?

1. Inquiry Skill Practice–Make a Model

Think of a tower of blocks as a model of an ecosystem. Each block is a population of animals or plants. What do you think would happen if one important population of animals or plants vanished from the ecosystem?

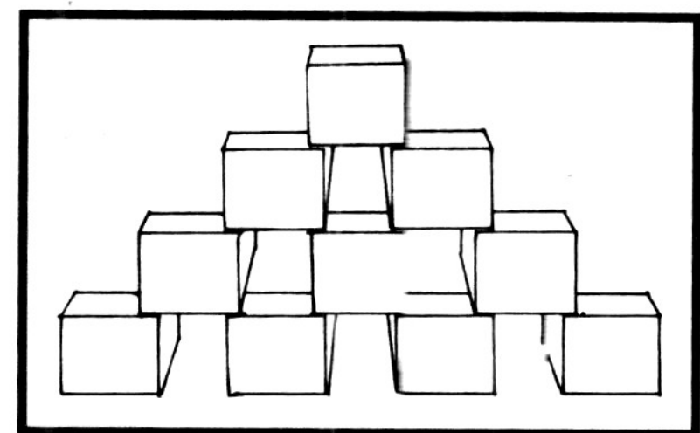

____

2. Use Vocabulary

Match the clue on the left to the term on the right.

	Clue		Term
____	A group of organisms of the same kind that live in the same place	**A.**	ecosystem
____	The living and nonliving things in an environment that interact	**B.**	population
____	All of the populations that live in an ecosystem at the same time	**C.**	community

3.  Reading Skill Practice–Main Idea and Details

Read the selection. Underline the main idea. List at least two details.

An ecosystem is all the living and nonliving things that interact in an environment. Imagine a small pond. Fish live in the water. Frogs jump from lily pad to lily pad. Fish, frogs, and ducks feed from animals and plants that live by the pond. All the animals and plants interact, breathe the same air, and use the same water. That small pond is an ecosystem.

____

Name ______________________________

4. Focus Skill **Main Idea and Details**

Complete the graphic organizer. List details about an ecosystem.

Main Idea: A pond ecosystem is made up of living and nonliving things.

Living Things	Nonliving Things
A ______________________	B ______________________

5. **Critical Thinking and Problem Solving**

Sometimes we do things that can help or destroy the habitats of animals. What are some things we can do to help protect their habitats rather than destroy them?

____

____

____

Name ______________________________

Date ______________________________

Lesson 2 - What Factors Influence Ecosystems?

1. Inquiry Skill Practice–Compare

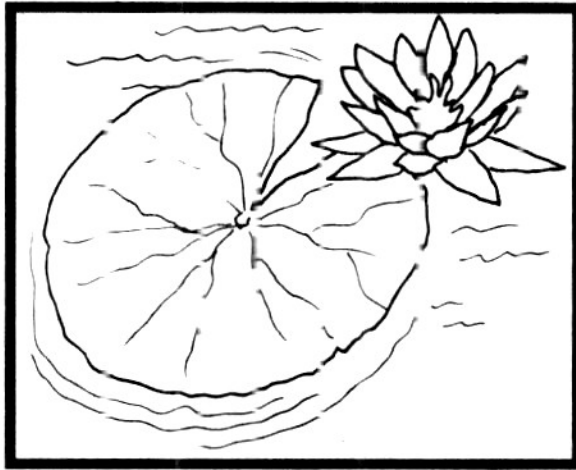

Both plants in the drawing rely on abiotic factors to survive in their ecosystem. However, neither plant would survive in the ecosystem of the other. What makes each plant's ecosystem suitable for its survival?

____

2. Use Vocabulary

Complete each sentence with the correct term from the box.

biotic
abiotic
diversity

_______________ factors are the living things in an ecosystem.

The number of different kinds of living things are referred to as _______________.

_______________ factors are the nonliving things in an ecosystem.

3. Focus Skill Reading Skill Practice–Cause and Effect

Read the selection. Describe the cause and effect.

What we do affects the ecosystem around us. Imagine a wooded area. There are birds, squirrels, raccoons, and other animals that live there. They use the lake in the wooded area to drink, feed, and even bathe. People start to walk by and enjoy the view. Each time a person passes by he drops an empty bottle or can, or any other piece of garbage. The lake and wooded area start to get dirty. The animals that depend on the lake and the woods can no longer use it safely. They start to get sick and die. Many others go away. The ecosystem vanishes.

____

Name ______________________________

4. **Focus Skill** **Cause and Effect**

Use this space to complete the graphic organizer shown in the Reading Review of the Student Edition.

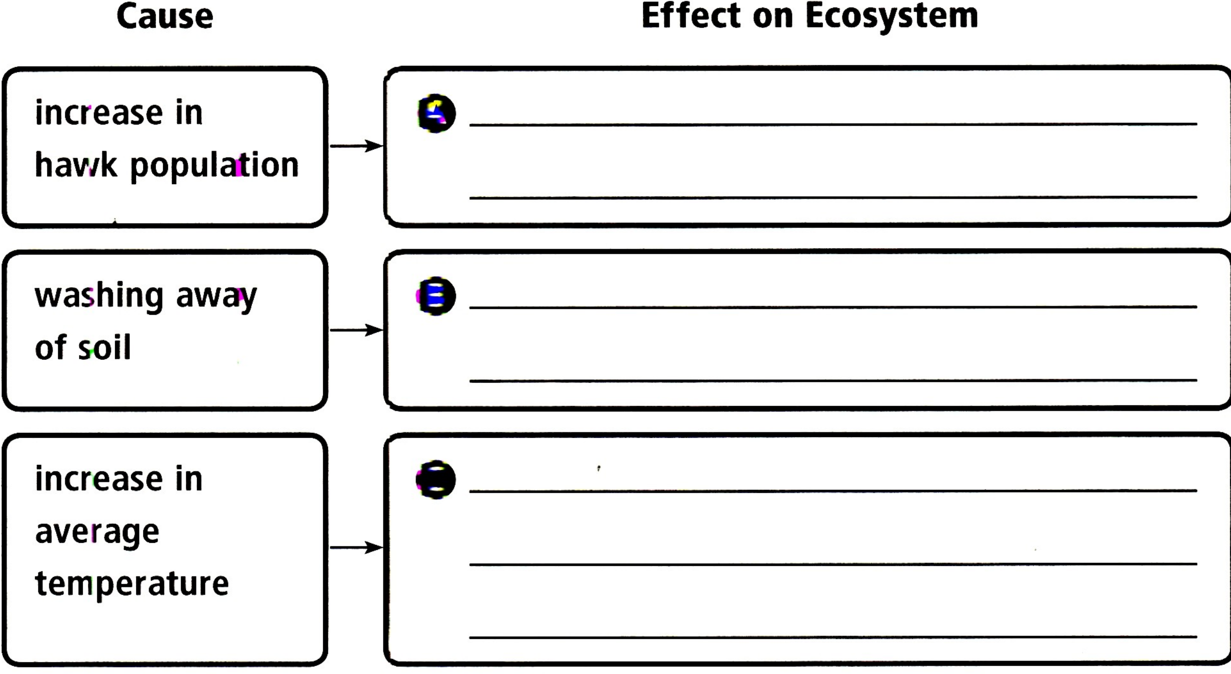

Cause	Effect on Ecosystem
increase in hawk population	______________________________
washing away of soil	______________________________
increase in average temperature	______________________________

5. **Critical Thinking and Problem Solving**

What are the biotic and abiotic factors that support the ecosystem where you live? How do the biotic factors rely on the abiotic factors to live?

____

____

____

Name ______________________________

Date ______________________________

Lesson 4 - How Do Humans Affect Ecosystems?

1. **Inquiry Skill Practice–Experiment**

Design an experiment to test how much garbage your classroom generates.

____

2. **Use Vocabulary**

Complete each sentence with the correct term from the box.

pollution
habitat restoration

The fumes coming from cars are raising the level of ________________.

The children of the town are planning a __________________ by planting many trees in the nearby landfill.

3. Focus Skill **Reading Skill Practice–Compare and Contrast**

Read the selection. Compare and contrast Lina and Olga's actions.

Lina and Olga agree to meet by the seashore. Lina asks her parents to drop her off. Olga walks to meet Lina. After they meet, they walk along the seashore. Lina drops an empty bottle on the sand. Olga disposes of Lina's bottle correctly. Lina and Olga see a small plant growing near a soiled part of the beach. Lina tries to take it. Olga stops her and reminds her that plants are part of nature, and nature should not be destroyed.

____

____

____

Name ______________________________

4. Focus Skill **Compare and Contrast**

Complete the graphic organizer.

Human Effects on Ecosystems	
Negative Change: destruction of habitats	**Positive Change: Ⓐ ______________**
Negative Change: Ⓑ ______________	**Positive Change: devices to reduce air pollution from cars**

5. **Critical Thinking and Problem Solving**

In most areas of the United States, there are efforts to preserve the environment. What are the natural areas near you that people are working to protect? In what ways are these efforts successful?

____

____

____

Name ______________________________

Date ______________________________

Energy Transfer in Ecosystems

A. Suffixes

Adding a suffix to a word changes its meaning and usage. The suffix *–er* and *–or* often stands for "one who" or "one that." Use the words in the box to write the words defined below.

consumer	decomposer	predator	producer

1. one who produces ______________
2. one who consumes ______________
3. one that preys or destroys ______________
4. one that decomposes or breaks down ______________

B. Related Words

There are three kinds of consumers—herbivores, carnivores, and omnivores. The word part *vore* means "one who eats or feeds on." The prefix of the words tells you what they eat. Write the related words for the clues below.

5. Who would feed on just plants? ______________
6. Who would feed on meat? ______________
7. Who would feed on both meat and plants? ______________

Name ______________________

Date ______________________

Lesson Quick Study

Lesson 1 - What are the Roles of Living Things?

1. **Inquiry Skill Practice–Infer**

Draw lines to match each animal to its food. What can you infer about each animal?

2. **Use Vocabulary**

Match the clue on the left to the term on the right. Write the letter in the blank.

____ organism that can make its own food	**A.**	decomposer
____ organism that eats plants or other organisms	**B.**	consumer
____ organism that feeds on wastes and plant and animal remains	**C.**	producer

3. 

Reading Skill Practice–Main Idea and Details

Read the selection. Underline the main idea. Circle at least three details about the main idea.

Producers are organisms that make their own food. These organisms are very important. Producers can be found in many places. In the ocean, you can find producers such as seaweed. In deserts, there are cacti and shrubs. In forests, we find trees and moss. Where else can we find producers?

Name ______________________________

4. Focus Skill **Main Idea and Details**

Use this space to complete the graphic organizer shown in the Reading Review of the Student Edition.

Main Idea: All living things are producers, consumers, or decomposers.

Producers	Consumers	Decomposers
green plants	herbivores	
A	B	D
	C	

5. **Critical Thinking and Problem Solving**

How are the decomposers in an environment helpful to the consumers in the environment?

____

____

____

____

____

Name ______________________

Date ______________________

Lesson 2 - How Do Living Things Get Energy?

1. Inquiry Skills Practice–Communicate

Think about the living things that live in your community. Complete the table below to communicate information about these living things and their habitats. An example has been done for you.

Living Thing	Description	Habitat
squirrel	gray-brown fur, 4 legs, bushy tail	trees

2. Use Vocabulary

Complete each sentence with a word from the box.

habitat
prey
predators
food web

Consumers that eat prey are called ______________.

The ocean is the ______________ of many fish.

A ______________ is a group of food chains that overlap.

Consumers that are eaten are called ______________.

3. Focus Skill — Reading Skill Practice–Sequence

Put the following events in a food chain in the correct sequence. Number the events 1 to 3.

____ A bird feeds on the grasshopper that fed on grass.

____ A grasshopper feeds on grass.

____ A cat feeds on the bird that fed on the grasshopper that fed on grass.

Name ______________________________

4. Focus Skill Sequence

Use this space to complete the graphic organizer shown in the Reading Review of the Student Edition.

Put the words below in order to create a food chain.

woodpecker	leaves	insect	hawk

A. → B. → C. → D.

5. Critical Thinking and Problem Solving

You learned that in a food chain there are producers, different levels of consumers, and decomposers. Draw an example of each group. Draw the pictures in their order in the food chain. Label each picture.

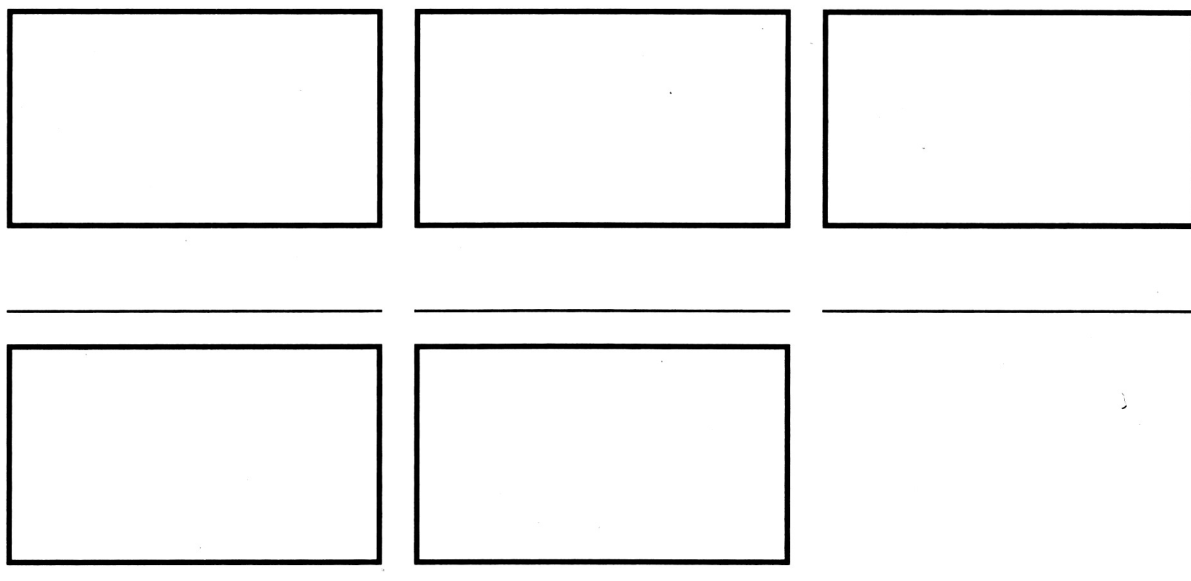

Name ______________________________

Date ______________________________

Write a Story About Earth's Layers

Narrative Writing–Story

Imagine that you are able to travel in a protected glass elevator from the surface of the Earth to the planet's core. Write a story about what you see as you travel. Use colorful, descriptive language to describe Earth's layers as accurately as you can. Use the story map below to help you plan your writing.

Describe the setting (glass elevator):
What do you see as you descend?
What do you see when the elevator reaches the planet's core?
What was your favorite part of the journey?

Name ______________________

Date ______________________

The Rock Cycle

A. Explore Word Meanings

Think about the meaning of the underlined words. Then write your answer to each question.

1. A mineral is a solid substance that occurs naturally in rocks or in the ground. Which of the following would be a mineral—oil or gold?

   ____

2. An igneous rock forms when melted rock cools and hardens. Where might you find an igneous rock—near a volcano or near an iceberg?

   ____

3. A sedimentary rock forms when pieces of rocks are broken down and moved. The broken down rocks pile up in layers and are squeezed together. What might cause a rock to break down—wind or sunlight?

   ____

4. A metamorphic rock forms when heat and pressure change an existing rock. What might cause a metamorphic rock to form—ocean waves or mountain building?

   ____

5. Weathering is the breaking down of rocks on Earth's surface into smaller particles. What might cause weathering to occur—rainwater or pollution?

   ____

6. Erosion is the process of moving sediment from one place to another. What might cause erosion to occur—magnets or glaciers?

   ____

Name ______________________________

Date ______________________________

Lesson Quick Study

Lesson 1 - What Are the Types of Rocks?

1. **Inquiry Skill Practice–Use Models/Compare**

Gina pours some sugar in a hot pan. The sugar melts. She places the pan with the melted sugar in a cool place. The sugar hardens in one single piece. How does Gina's model compare to the way an actual igneous rock would form?

____

____

____

2. **Use Vocabulary**

Matching: Match the clue on the left to the term on the right.

____	Rock formed from heat and pressure	**A.**	metamorphic
____	Rock forms from pressed layers of broken pieces of rocks	**B.**	rock
____	Rock melts, cools, and hardens	**C.**	igneous
____	A solid substance made of minerals	**D.**	sedimentary

3. Focus Skill **Reading Skill Practice–Main Idea and Details**

Read the selection. Underline the main idea. List at least 3 details.

Igneous rock is one of three groups of rocks. It forms when melted rock cools and hardens. This melted rock called magma is deep inside the earth. There, temperatures are so hot that rock is liquid. When magma reaches Earth's surface, it cools and becomes hard.

____

____

Name ______________________________

4. **Main Idea and Details**

Use this space to complete the graphic organizer shown in the Reading Review of the Student Edition.

Fill in the graphic organizer below.

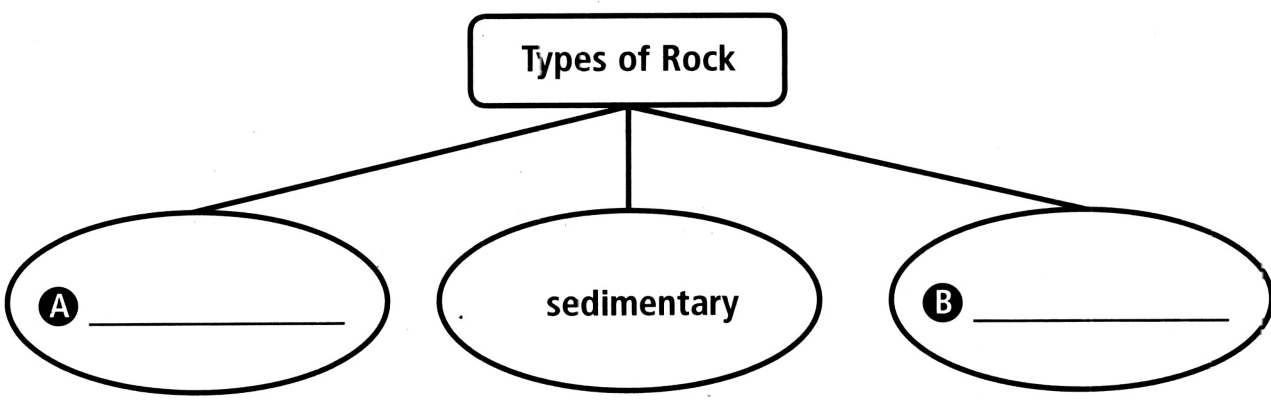

5. **Critical Thinking and Problem Solving**

Imagine you could use a movie camera to record how a rock undergoes changes. A rock starts out as an igneous rock. Water and wind break the rock down into small pieces. They carry the small pieces of rock to the surface of the ocean and pile them up into layers. What might the camera record next? Explain.

____

____

____

____

____

Name ______________________________

Date ______________________________

Lesson Quick Study

Lesson 2 - What Is the Rock Cycle?

1. Inquiry Skill Practice—Plan and Conduct a Simple Investigation

Suppose you are going to **conduct a simple investigation** to find out about the types of rocks in your area. Which of the following is a better **plan** for finding this information? Explain your answer.

Take a walk and collect different rocks from your area. Remember where you found them. Sort the rocks by size when you get home.	Take a walk and collect different rocks from your area. Record where you found them. Sort the rocks by color, hardness, and grain size.

____

____

2. Use Vocabulary

Write a complete sentence that uses the words *rock cycle* correctly.

____

3. Focus Skill Reading Skill Practice—Sequence

Put the following events about the rock cycle in the correct sequence. Number the steps 1 to 5.

____ High heat and pressure act on the sandstone, turning it into quartzite.

____ The quartzite hardens into andesite.

____ Sandstone gets pushed into Earth's crust during mountain building.

____ After time, the quartzite cools.

____ The quartzite melts after undergoing even more heat and pressure.

Name ________________________________

4. Focus Skill **Sequence**

Use this space to complete the graphic organizer shown in the Reading Review of the Student Edition.

Fill in the graphic organizer below.

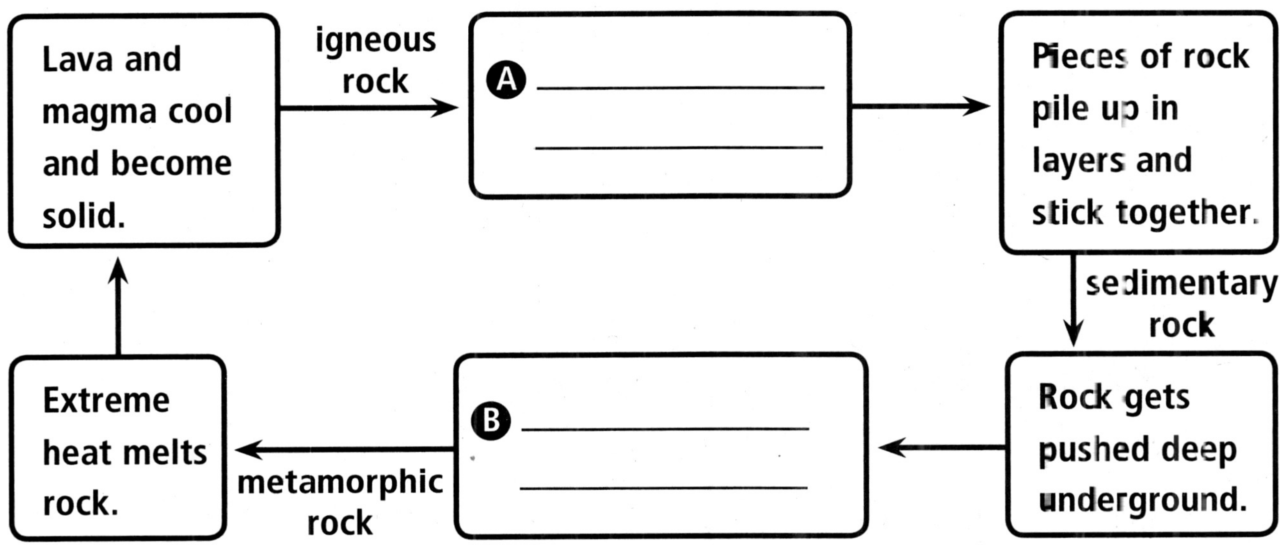

5. **Critical Thinking and Problem Solving**

Which rock do you think would be harder to break with a hammer: a sedimentary rock or an igneous rock? Explain.

____

____

____

____

____

Name ______________________

Date ______________________

Lesson 3 - How Do Weathering and Erosion Affect Rocks?

1. **Inquiry Skills Practice—Infer**

Limestone is a sedimentary rock. It forms partly from seashells that have been broken down and squeezed together. What can you infer caused the seashells to break into pieces?

____

____

2. **Use Vocabulary**

Rock breaking down into smaller pieces is called ______________.

Sediment moving from one place to another is called ______________.

weathering
erosion

3. 

Reading Skill Practice–Cause and Effect

Read the selection. Describe the cause and effect of weathering.

Many factors cause weathering. It happens all around us. Suppose a large rock has a small crack. Now suppose a bird carries a seed as it flies above the rock. The seed drops from the bird's beak and falls into the rock crack. With time, the seed grows into a plant. The growing plant's roots expand, breaking the rock even further. Time continues to pass and winter arrives. It rains. Water gets into the crack. The water freezes. As the water freezes, it expands. The crack continues to expand. Before you know it, the large rock with a small crack becomes a small rock with a large crack.

____

____

Name ______________________________

4. Focus Skill **Cause and Effect**

Use this space to complete the graphic organizer shown in the Reading Review of the Student Edition.

Fill in the graphic organizer below.

Causes of Weathering

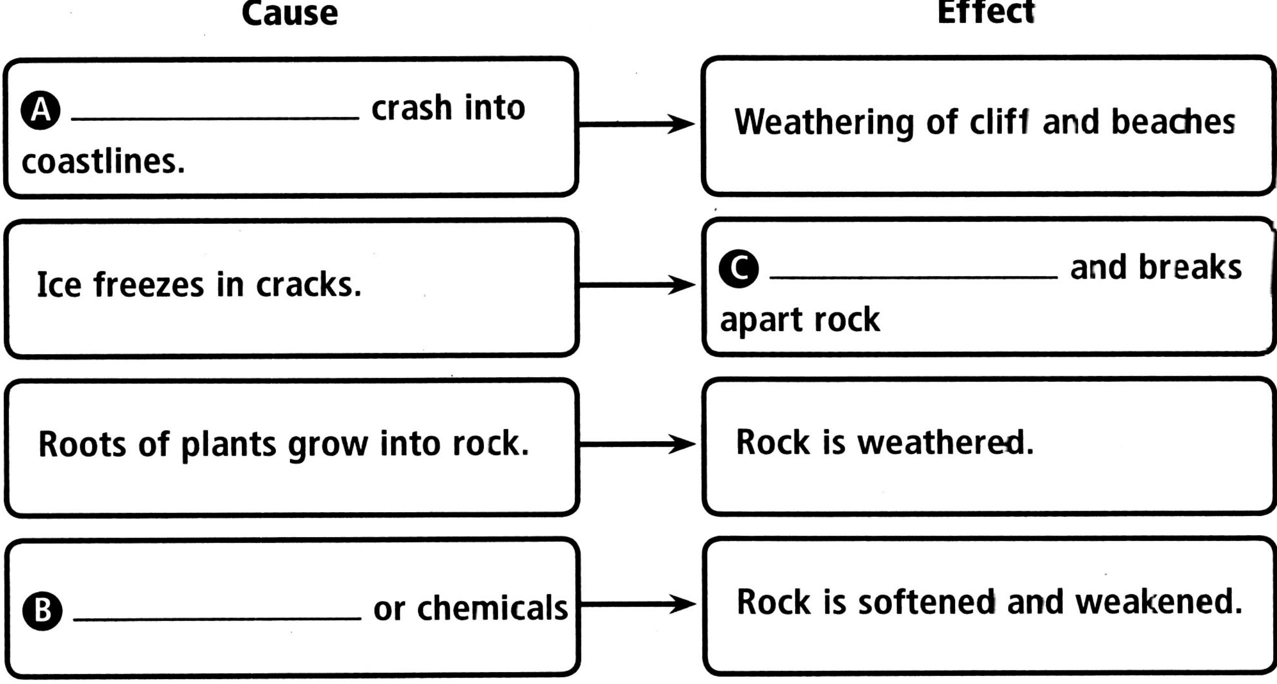

5. **Critical Thinking and Problem Solving**

Imagine there are heavy rainfalls for days. The river near the area starts to overflow. Erosion starts to take place. Explain what happens.

____

____

____

____

Name ______________________

Date ______________________

Lesson Quick Study

Lesson 4 - What Is Soil?

1. Inquiry Skill Practice–Compare

Soil A

Sand

Soil B

Clay

Look at the two containers with soil. Compare the types of soil. What do you think will happen if you plant a seed in each one of them?

____

____

____

2. Use Vocabulary

humus
horizon
bedrock
sand
clay

Complete each sentence with the correct term from the box.

The largest particle that makes up soil is ______________.

The smallest particle that makes up soil is ______________.

Most soils are made up of ______________ or layers.

The remains of decayed plants and animals are called ______________.

The solid rock that forms Earth's surface is called ______________.

3.  Reading Skill Practice–Compare and Contrast

Read the selection. Compare and contrast the types of soils.

Janet buys two types of soils to plant a garden. One type of soil is gritty. It absorbs water very fast. This soil has large grains. The other type of soil is spongy. Water is not absorbed fast. It lingers in the soil. This soil has small grains.

____

____

Name ______________________________

4. **Compare and Contrast**

Complete the graphic organizer.

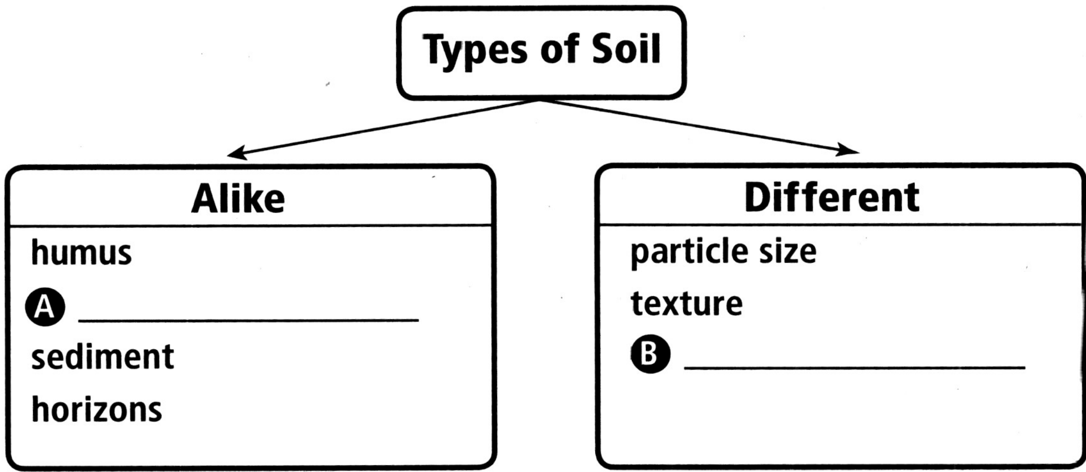

5. **Critical Thinking and Problem Solving**

How can a fertilizer help plants grow? Explain.

____

____

____

____

Name ______________________________

Date ______________________________

Vocabulary Power

Changes to Earth's Surface

A. Compound Words

Compound words are made up of two words. The two words may be joined together, hyphenated, or kept separate. Read the words below and write the two words that make up the compound word. Then use the Glossary to write the definition for each compound word.

1. earthquake ______________

____

2. fossil record ______________

____

3. landform ______________

____

B. Explore Word Meanings

Read each statement. Draw a picture of each underlined word.

4. Travelers aboard a cruise ship took pictures of a <u>glacier</u>. Draw a picture of what a glacier looks like.

5. Construction workers found animal <u>fossils</u> embedded in rocks. Draw a picture of an animal fossil.

Name ______________________

Date ______________________

Lesson 1 - What Are Some of Earth's Landforms?

1. **Inquiry Skill Practice–Observe and Use a Model**

Observe each one of the models below. Write *river, lake,* and *ocean* to show which mass of water each model might represent.

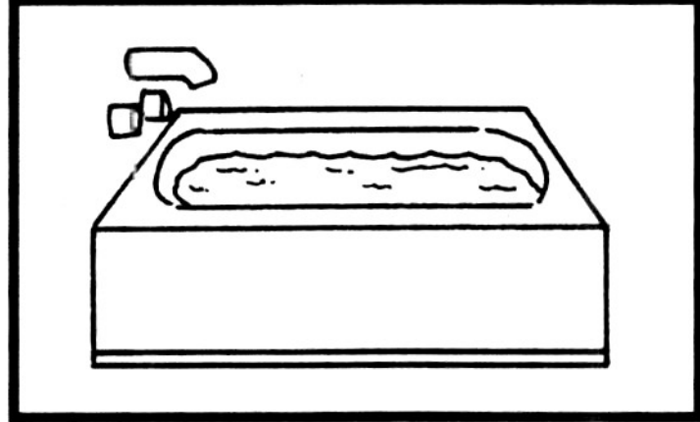

______________ ______________ ______________

2. **Use Vocabulary**

Complete each sentence with the correct term from the box.

landform mountain topography

The shape of the landform in an area is called ______________. A ______________ is an area that is higher than the area around it. A natural feature in Earth's surface is called a ______________.

3. Focus Skill **Reading Skill Practice–Compare and Contrast**

Read the selection. Compare and contrast farming on mountains and plains.

Farming on mountains is not like farming on plains. Plains have wide, flat land. Farmers use machines and animals to help them plant and grow large crops. Farmers who live on mountains build steps called terraces on the sides of the mountain. Each terrace is a narrow

(cont'd.)

Name ______________________________

bed of soil for growing crops. Terrace farming is done largely by hand, since farmers cannot carry machines from step to step.

____

____

4. **Compare and Contrast**

Complete the graphic organizer.

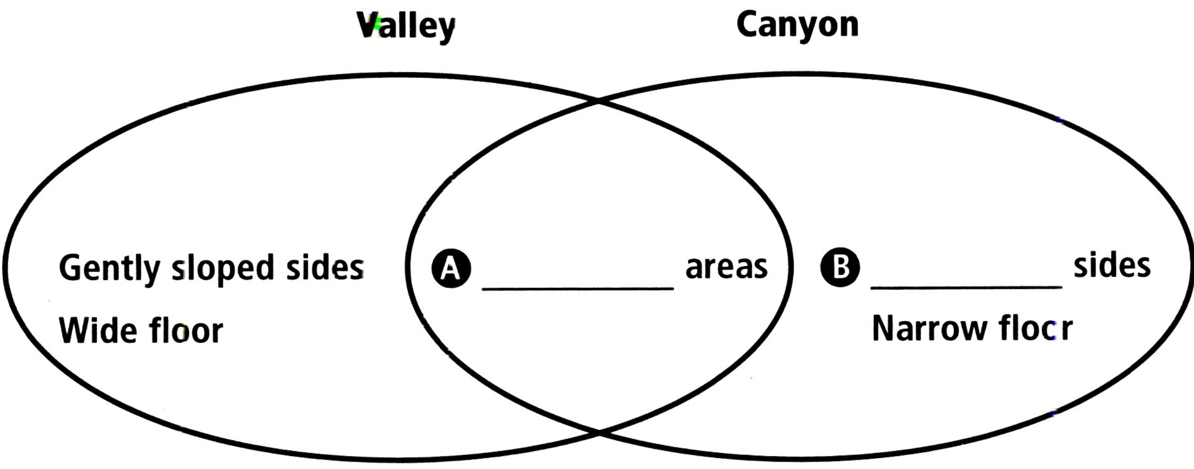

5. **Critical Thinking and Problem Solving**

Suppose you want to go hiking. You want to climb to the highest areas and explore the lowest ones of your destination. Where will you go—a plain, a valley, or a plateau? Explain.

____

____

____

____

____

____

Name ______________________________

Date ______________________________

Lesson Quick Study

Lesson 2 - What Causes Changes to Earth's Landforms?

1. Inquiry Skill Practice—Make a Model

Suppose you use a peach to model the parts of Earth. Label the peach to show what part of the peach represents what part of Earth.

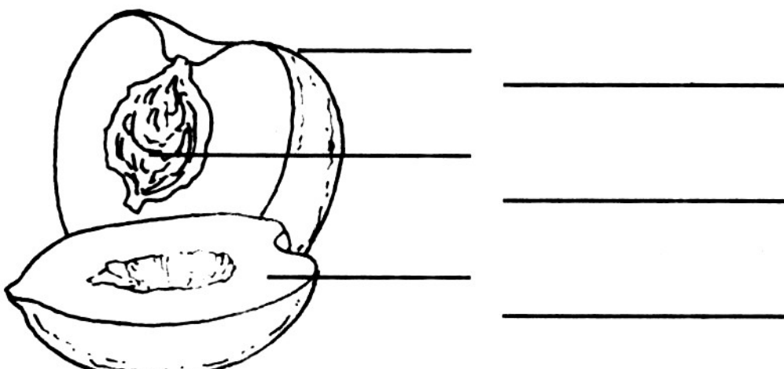

____

____

____

2. Use Vocabulary

Match the clue on the left to the term on the right.

____ This occurs when rivers drop bits of rocks and soils.

____ They are made of layers of lava, rock, and ash.

____ This causes shaking, rolling, and cracking in the crust and Earth's surface.

____ These are large moving blocks of ice.

A. volcano

B. earthquake

C deposition

D. glacier

3. Focus Skill Reading Skill Practice—Cause and Effect

Read the selection. Underline the cause of earthquakes. Circle the effects.

Earthquakes can occur suddenly. They can damage land and buildings. Their results could be deadly. An earthquake occurs when Earth's crust is broken into plates. These plates move towards each other. They slide past each other along these breaks. Sometimes rocks from two different plates stick together along a fault. Great pressure can build up in these rocks, causing the rocks to break apart suddenly. This releases waves of energy, causing the plates to move with a sudden shake.

Name ___________________________

4. **Cause and Effect**

Complete the graphic organizer.

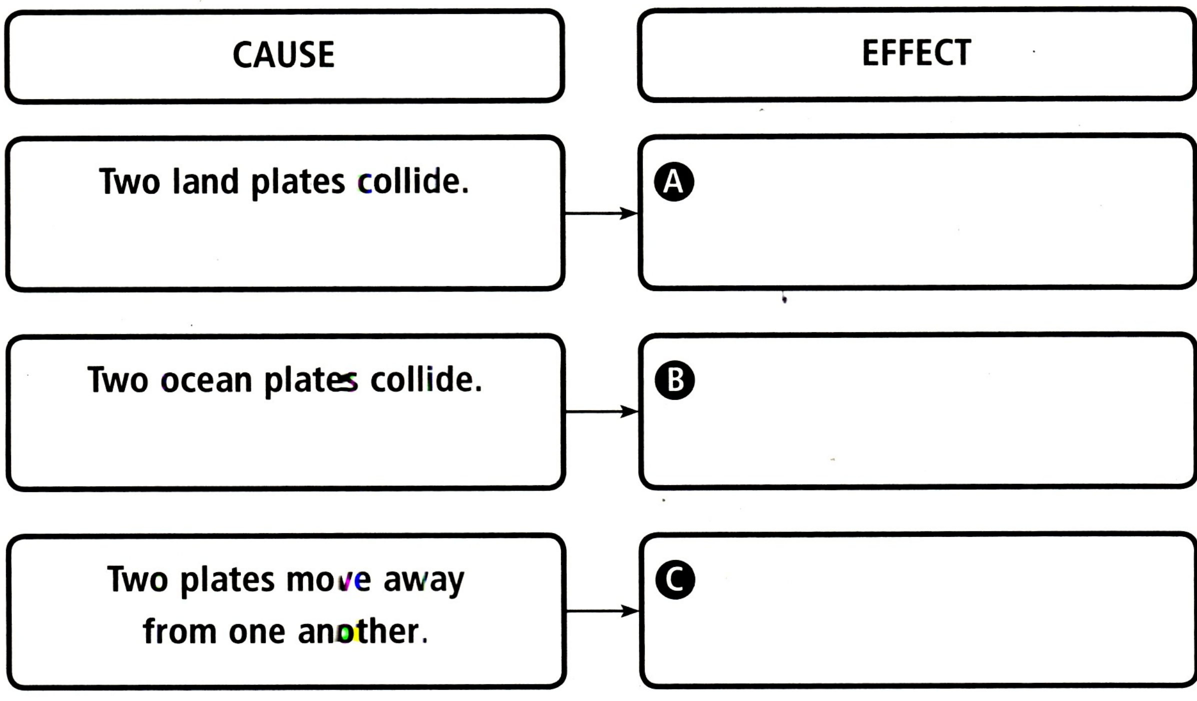

CAUSE	EFFECT
Two land plates collide.	A
Two ocean plates collide.	B
Two plates move away from one another.	C

5. **Critical Thinking and Problem Solving**

Suppose you live on a volcanic island. What do you suppose are the dangers and hardships of living there?

____

____

____

____

Name ______________________________

Date ______________________________

Lesson 3 - What Are Fossils?

1. Inquiry Skill Practice–Predict

Imagine a populated lake area filled with aquatic animals. Something strange happens and everyone leaves the area. The lake starts to dry up. Millions of years pass. Scientists return to the lake area and start to dig where the lake once was. Predict what they would find.

____

____

2. Use Vocabulary

Write a complete sentence that uses the word *fossil* correctly.

____

Write a complete sentence that uses the word *fossil record* correctly.

____

3. Focus Skill Reading Skill Practice–Sequence

Put the following events about the formation of a clam fossil in the correct sequence. Number the steps 1 to 4.

____ The soft part of the clam decays.

____ The mold fills with minerals.

____ Its shell leaves a clam-shaped hole in the sedimentary rock called a mold.

____ Sediment covers a clam.

Name ______________________________

4. Focus Skill **Sequence**

Use this space to complete the graphic organizer shown in the Reading Review of the Student Edition.

Fill in the graphic organizer below.

What Are the Steps of Fossil Formation?
Step 1 A small sea animal with a shell (A) ______________________________
↓
Step 2 Soft parts of the animal decay.
↓
Step 3 A space forms in the rock where the soft parts used to be.
↓
Step 4 Minerals fill the space.
↓
Step 5 (B) ______________________________ forms in the rock.

5. **Critical Thinking and Problem Solving**

Some fossils of shells and fish have been found at the tops of rocky mountain peaks. How do you suppose this happened?

____

____

____

____

Name ______________________________

Date ______________________________

Compare and Contrast

The moon's gravity pulls on the ocean and causes tides. The sun's gravity does the same, but because the sun is so far away, its pull is less than half that of the moon. Sometimes, during a new or full moon, when the sun and the moon are lined up, their forces are added together. When this happens, the gravitational pull on tides gets stronger. Write a paragraph that compares and contrasts the effects of the moon's gravity and the sun's gravity on the ocean's tides. Use the Venn diagram below to help you plan your paragraph.

Write About Tides

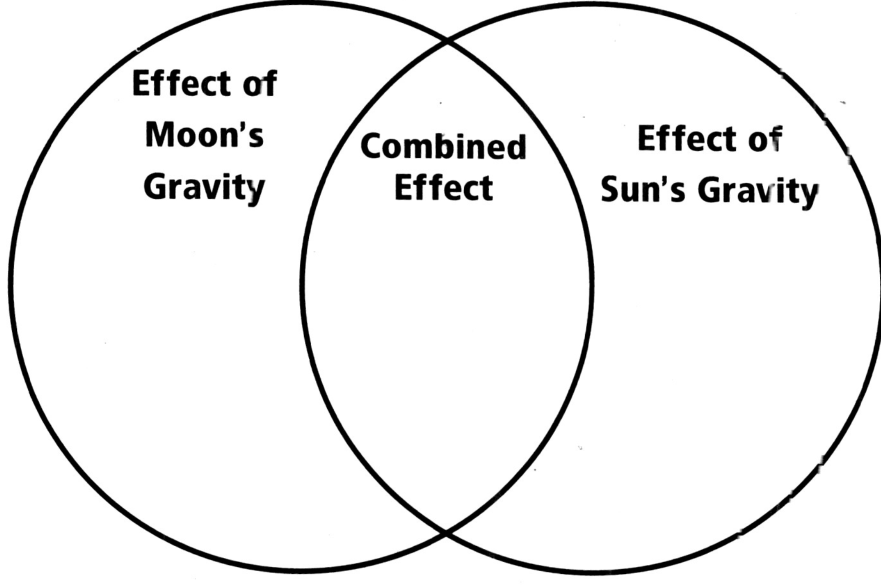

My paragraph: ____

____

____

____

____

____

____

Name ______________________
Date ______________________

The Water Cycle

A. Classifying Words

A word map can show how words are related to each other. Read the words in the box. Then look at the word map. Add words from the box to the word map by writing each word near the word it is most closely related to. One has been done for you.

air mass	anemometer	barometer	cold front
condensation	evaporation	hail	hurricane
land breeze	rain	rain shadow	sea breeze
sleet	snow	tornado	warm front

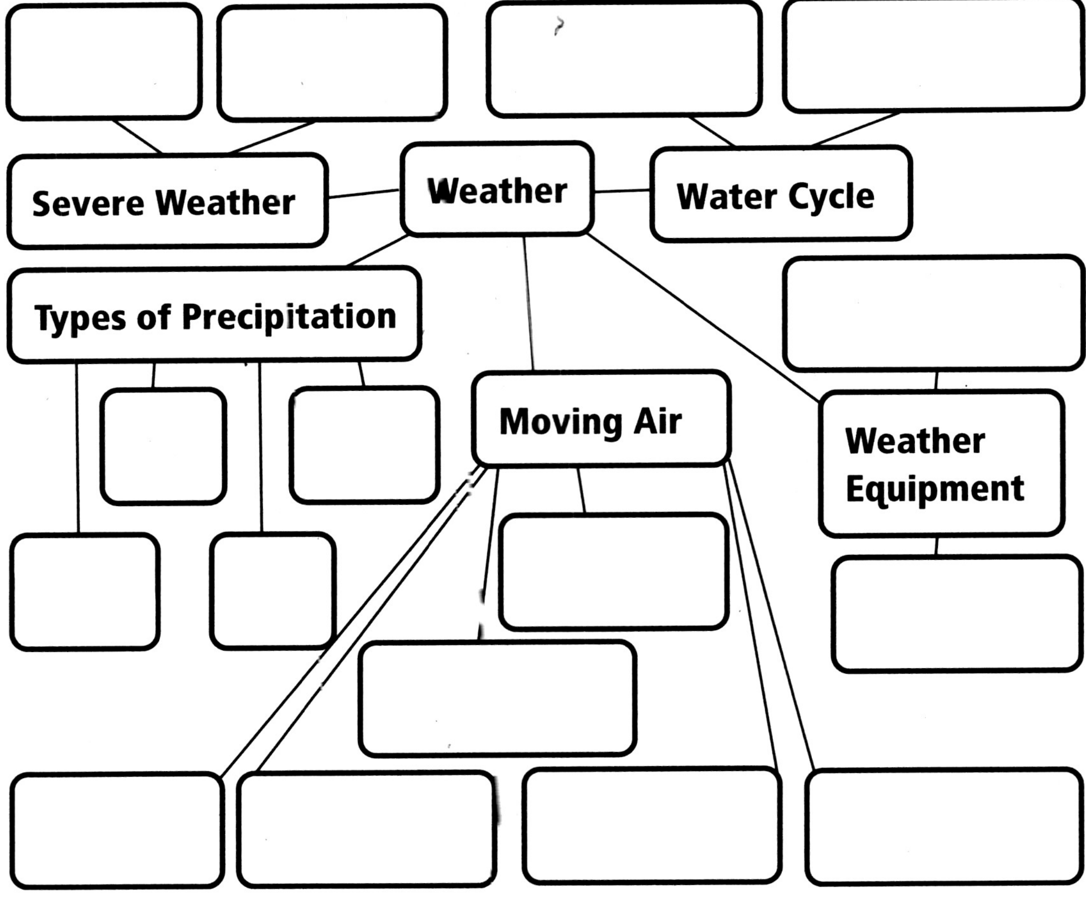

Name ______________________________
Date ______________________________

Lesson 1 - What Is the Water Cycle?

1. Inquiry Skills Practice–Infer

Suppose you water your front garden on a hot, sunny day. The sidewalk gets soaked as you water the garden. A few hours later, the sidewalk is dry.

What do you infer happened to the water that was on the sidewalk?

____

____

____

2. Use Vocabulary

Complete each sentence with the correct term from the box.

precipitation evaporation condensation

The water droplets on the outer part of a cold drink glass are an example of ________________.

________________ helps plants grow and rivers flow.

________________ is what dries the dew on the grass.

3. Focus Skill Reading Skill Practice–Sequence

Put the following events in the water cycle in the correct sequence. Number the events 1 to 5.

____ Water vapor cools and turns to liquid water.

____ Liquid water falls back to Earth.

____ Water changes from liquid to water vapor.

____ Energy from the sun warms water on Earth's surface.

____ Water vapor goes into the air.

Name ___________________________

4. Focus Skill **Sequence**

Use this space to complete the graphic organizer shown in the Reading Review of the Student Edition.

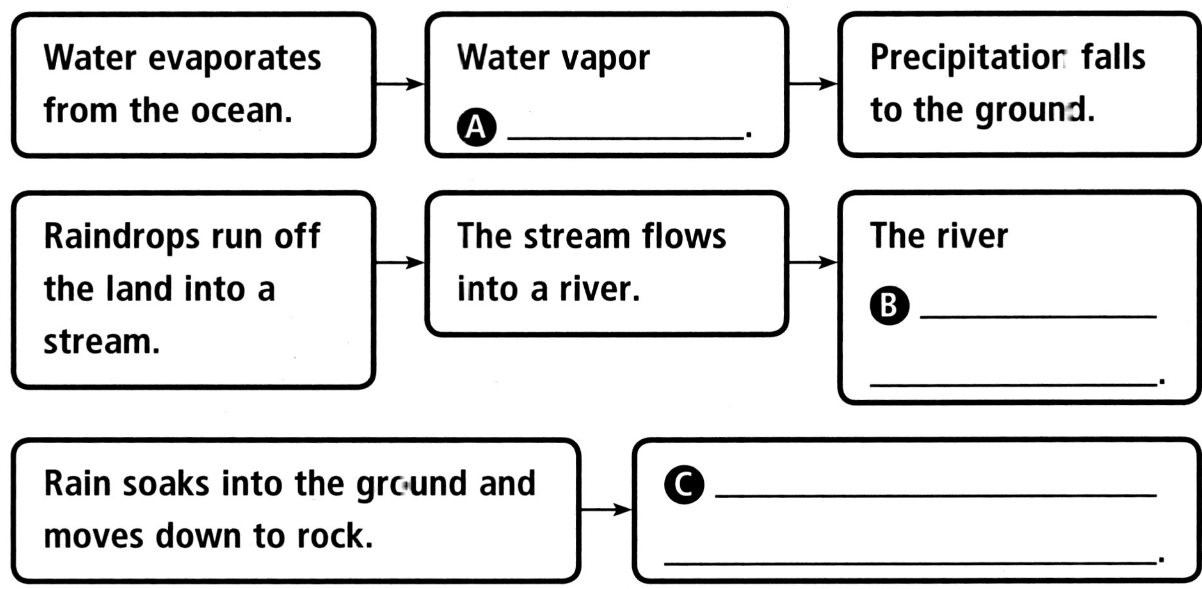

5. **Critical Thinking and Problem Solving**

Not all of the water that falls as rain, snow, or sleet evaporates. What happens to the rest of the water?

____

____

____

____

____

____

____

Name ______________________________

Date ______________________________

Lesson 2 - How Is the Water Cycle Related to Weather?

1. **Inquiry Skill Practice–Gather, Record, Interpret Data**

Marlin is gathering, recording, and interpreting data about wind speeds, using a windsock near his home. Based on the sequence of illustrations, what could you interpret about the wind near Marlin's home today?

1

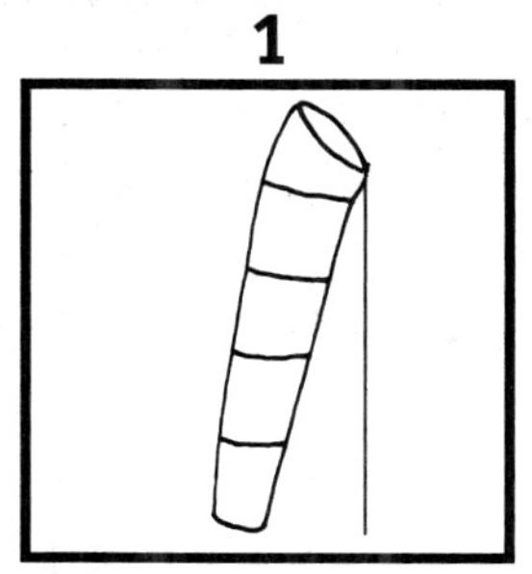

2

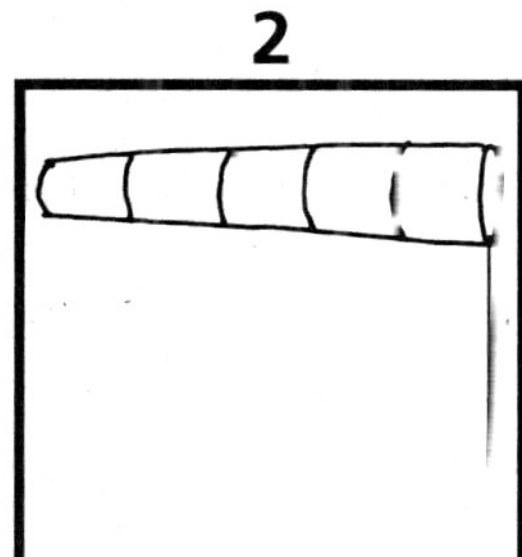

3

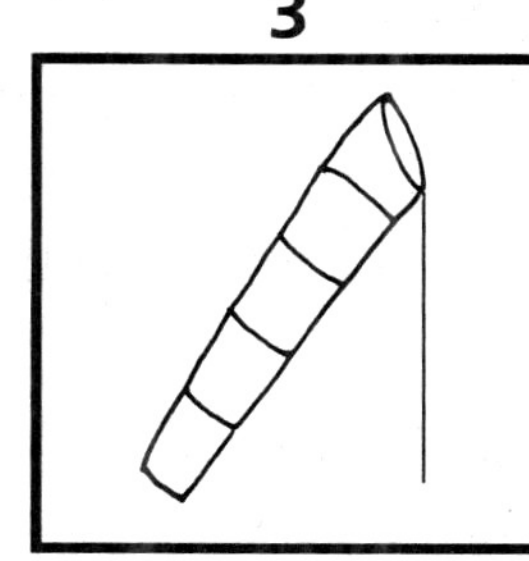

4

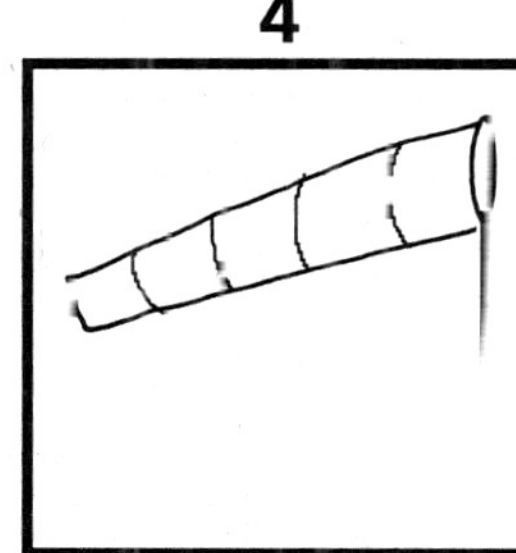

____

____

____

____

2. **Use Vocabulary**

Match the clue on the left to the term on the right. Write the letter in the blank.

____ frozen rain	**A.** rain
____ liquid water	**B.** snow
____ round pieces of ice	**C.** sleet
____ ice crystals	**D.** hail

3. Focus Skill **Reading Skill Practice–Cause and Effect**

Read the selection. Identify a cause and an effect described in it.

Tornadoes are destructive windstorms. A tornado's fast and powerful wind carries large objects into the air. These objects then

(cont'd.)

Name ______________________________

fall onto things like houses, trees, and roads, causing destruction. Tornadoes are dangerous, and we must be in a safe place while a tornado is near.

____

____

4. Focus Skill **Cause and Effect**

Complete the graphic organizer.

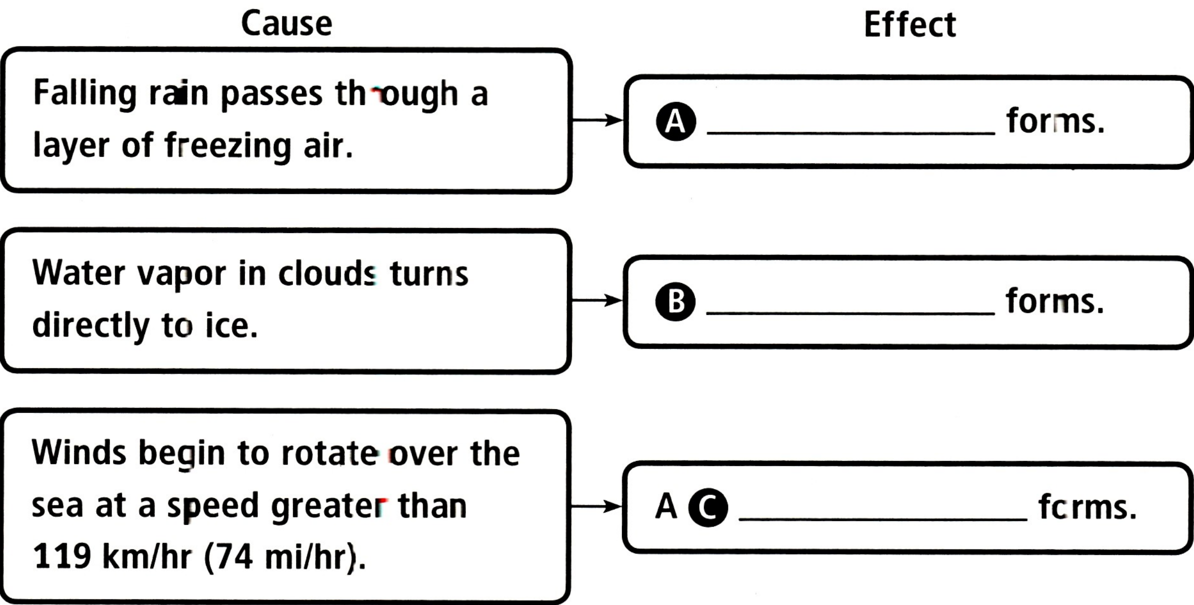

5. **Critical Thinking and Problem Solving**

Suppose rain starts to fall heavily. It does not stop for three days. What do you think the results might be? Who and what will be most affected by the results?

____

____

____

____

Name ________________________

Date ________________________

Lesson 3 - How Do Land Features Affect the Water Cycle?

1. **Inquiry Skills Practice–Form a Hypothesis**

Suppose you place a light bulb 12 inches above a pan filled with water. You place an identical light bulb 2 inches above an identical pan filled with water. Hypothesize which pan of water will heat up more quickly. Explain your reasoning.

____

____

2. **Use Vocabulary**

Write a complete sentence that uses the term correctly.

sea breeze: ________________________

land breeze: ________________________

3. Focus Skill **Reading Skill Practice–Cause and Effect**

Read the selection. Describe the cause and effect of rain in parts of Asia.

The monsoon winds have a strong effect on the climate in parts of Asia. For about six months, cool, dry winds blow down from the Himalayas and dry out the ground. Then the winds reverse direction and bring warm, wet air from the ocean. Heavy rains fall, and large areas flood. Agriculture in parts of Asia depends on monsoon rains. If the rains do not come, crops fail and people may starve.

____

____

Name ______________________________

4. Focus Skill **Cause and Effect**

Use this space to complete the graphic organizer shown in the Reading Review of the Student Edition.

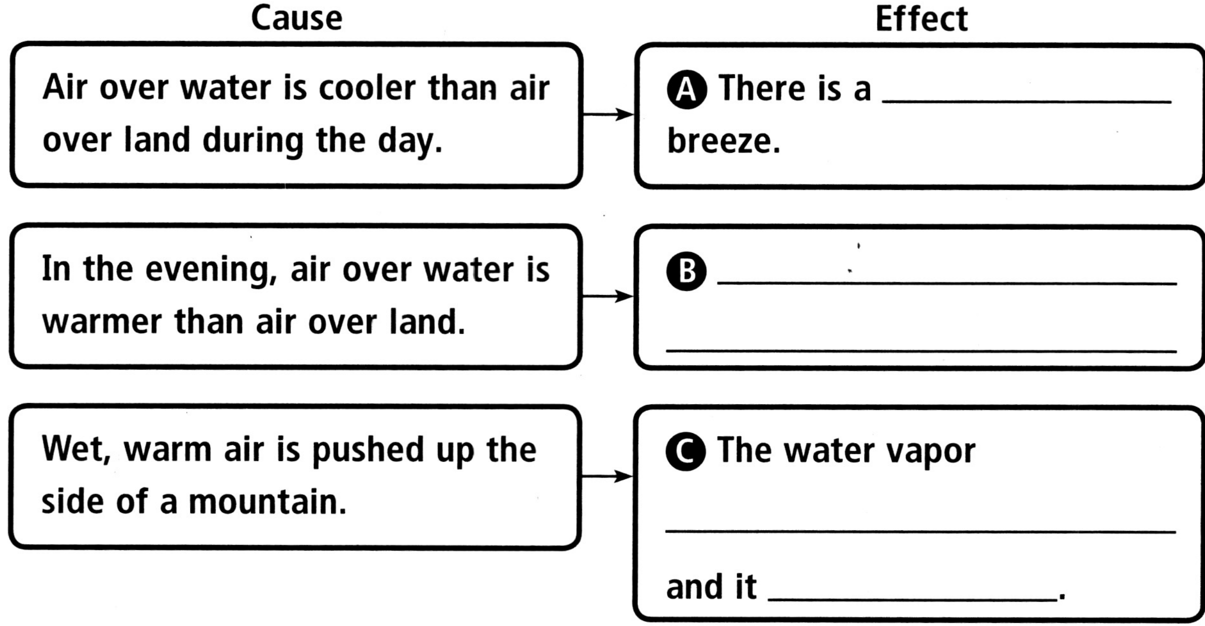

Cause		Effect
Air over water is cooler than air over land during the day.	→	A There is a ______________ breeze.
In the evening, air over water is warmer than air over land.	→	B ______________________ ______________________
Wet, warm air is pushed up the side of a mountain.	→	C The water vapor ______________________ and it ______________.

5. **Critical Thinking and Problem Solving**

In this lesson, you learned about rain shadows. You know that air can't move through a mountain. Instead, the air is pushed up the side of the mountain. As the air is pushed up, it cools. The water vapor in the cooler air condenses and brings rain to that side of the mountain. The air is dry once it reaches the other side of the mountain. It does not rain on that side. Draw a picture and label it to explain the process.

Name ______________________________

Date ______________________________

Lesson Quick Study

Lesson 4 - How Can Weather Be Predicted?

1. **Inquiry Skill Practice–Measure**

The weather instruments at your school make measurements using a thermometer, an anemometer, a barometer, and a rain gauge. If a cold front just moved over your area, do you think the measurements changed? How did they change?

____

____

2. **Use Vocabulary**

Complete each sentence with the correct term from the box.

air mass
cold front
barometer
anemometer

An ________________ is a tool used to measure wind speed.

A ________________ occurs when cold air moves under warm air.

An ________________ is a large body of air.

A ________________ is a tool used to measure air pressure.

3. Focus Skill **Reading Skill Practice–Cause and Effect**

Read the selection. Describe the cause and effect of cold weather in Florida.

A cold air mass forms in the northern part of North America. High winds blow the air mass toward the south. The air cools greatly. The cold air reaches Florida. The weather there gets colder than usual. Farmers light heaters and bonfires to keep oranges from freezing on the trees. Many oranges freeze anyway, and the crop is lost.

____

____

Name ______________________________

4. **Cause and Effect**

Use this space to complete the graphic organizer shown in the Reading Review of the Student Edition.

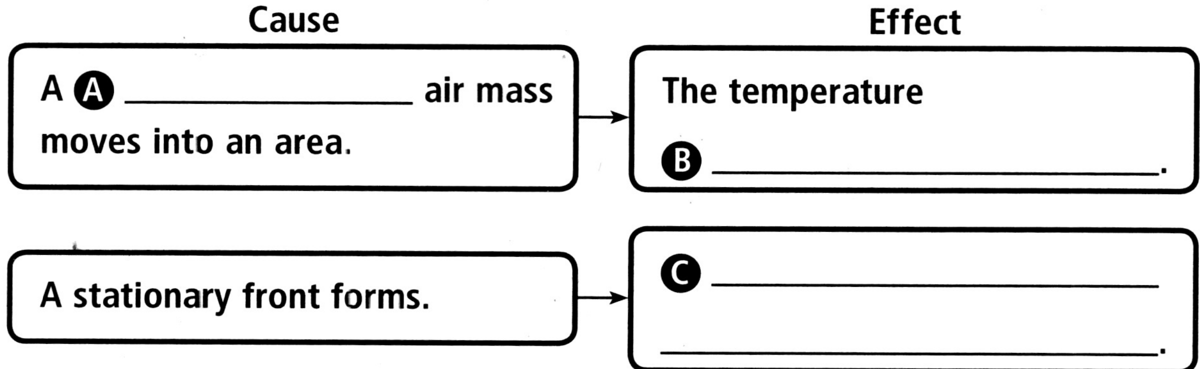

5. **Critical Thinking and Problem Solving**

Many people rely on the daily weather forecast to help plan their day. However, the forecast is sometimes incorrect. Can you think of a reason why the daily weather forecast might be wrong?

____

____

Name ______________________

Date ______________________

Planets and Other Objects in Space

A. Analogy

An analogy is made of two pairs of words. The words in each pair are related to each other in the same way. Think about the relationships in the following pairs of words. Then choose a word from the box to complete the analogy.

comet	galaxy	moon	orbit	sun

1. *Road* is to *highway* as *path* is to ______________.
2. *Sole* is to *pole* as *soon* is to ______________.
3. *Hubble* is to *telescope* as *Halley* is to ______________.
4. *Granny Smith* is to *apple* as *Milky Way* is to ______________.
5. *Won* is to *one* as *son* is to ______________.

B. Explore Word Meanings

Use the glossary to find the meaning of the underlined words. Then write your answer to each question.

6. A <u>solar system</u> is a group of objects in space that orbit around a star in the center. The center of our solar system is the sun. What does *solar* mean?

____

7. The <u>universe</u> is everything that exists in space. What are two examples of things in the universe?

____

Name ______________________________

Date ______________________________

Lesson 1 - How Do Earth and Its Moon Move?

1. Inquiry Skill Practice–Measure

December 32°F
January 30°F
February 34°F
June 79°F
July 85°F
August 87°F

Lupe measured and recorded the average temperatures during the day for the summer and winter months. What do you notice? What caused these temperature changes?

____

____

____

____

2. Use Vocabulary

Complete each sentence with the correct term from the box.

phases
orbits
axis
moon

When Earth moves around the sun, it ______________ the sun.

The moon has ______________ that follow a pattern, repeating about every $29\frac{1}{2}$ days.

The ______________ is the imaginary line from one pole of Earth to the other.

3. Reading Skill Practice–Sequence

Put the following events in the correct sequence. Number the events 1 to 3. Begin with the new moon phase.

____ More of the lit side of the moon is visible.

____ The entire lit side of the moon is visible from Earth.

____ None of the lit side of the moon is visible.

Name ______________________________

4. Focus Skill **Sequence**

Use this space to complete the graphic organizer shown in the Reading Review of the Student Edition.

winter solstice	spring Ⓐ ______________	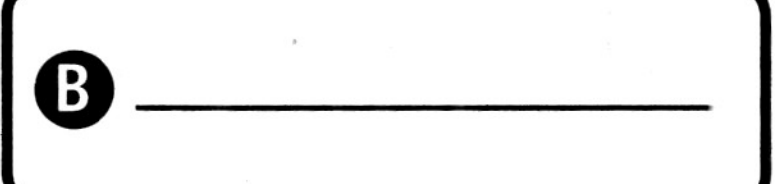 Ⓑ ______________	fall equinox

5. **Critical Thinking and Problem Solving**

Scientists often use models to study the movements of Earth and its moon. Why do you think they use models to study these movements?

____

____

____

Name ______________________________

Date ______________________________

Lesson Quick Study

Lesson 2 - How Do Objects Move in the Solar System?

1. **Inquiry Skill Practice–Use Numbers**

Use the numbers shown to draw a model of the order of the inner planets. Label the sun. Label each planet with a number. Use the space below to list the planets by number.

Planet	Distance from the Sun
Earth	149.6 million kilometers
Mars	227.9 million kilometers
Venus	108.2 million kilometers
Mercury	57.9 million kilometers

____

2. **Use Vocabulary**

Write a complete sentence that uses the terms *solar system, planets,* and *comets* correctly.

____

3. Focus Skill **Reading Skill Practice– Compare and Contrast**

Read the selection. Compare and contrast Mars and Earth.

Mars is an inner, rocky planet with no liquid water. Its diameter is about 6700 kilometers (4200 mi). Mars has two moons. Earth is an inner, rocky planet, with a surface that is 70 percent water. Earth's diameter is about 12,700 kilometers (7890 mi). It has one moon.

____

____

____

Name ______________________________

4. Compare and Contrast

Use this space to complete the graphic organizer shown in the Reading Review of the Student Edition.

Inner Planets

What's Different?

Close to (A) ______
Small with rocky surfaces
No more than ______ moons

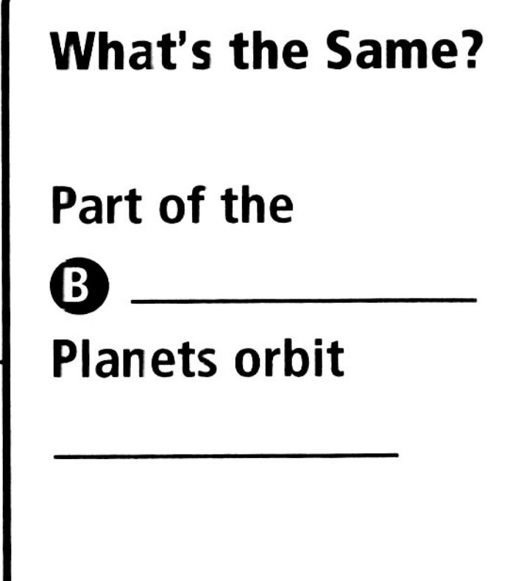

What's the Same?

Part of the (B) ______________
Planets orbit ______________

Outer Planets

What's Different?

(C) ______ from the sun
Have many ______
Rings of dust, ice, and rock
Large except for ______

5. Critical Thinking and Problem Solving

Mercury and Venus are the two planets closest to the sun. Venus has a thick atmosphere made of carbon dioxide. Mercury has a very thin atmosphere. Explain why Venus is hotter than Mercury, even though Mercury is closer to the sun.

____

____

____

Name ______________________

Date ______________________

Lesson 3 - What Other Objects Can Be Seen in the Sky?

1. **Inquiry Skills Practice–Plan an Investigation**

The drawing of Jupiter is based on a photograph taken through a telescope. Suppose you had a large telescope. Plan a simple investigation to study Jupiter. When and what would you study and investigate?

____

____

2. **Use Vocabulary**

Match the clue on the left to the term on the right. Write the letter in the blank.

____ a system made up of stars, gases, and dust — **A.** universe

____ star patterns that form an imaginary picture in the sky — **B.** galaxy

____ everything that exists in space — **C.** constellation

3. **Focus Skill** **Reading Skill Practice–Main Idea and Details**

Read the selection. Underline the main idea. List at least two details about the main idea.

In this lesson, you learned about groups of stars. Groups of stars can be classified in different ways. A group of stars can be known as a constellation. This is a pattern made by stars that form an imaginary picture in the sky. A galaxy is another kind of group of stars. A galaxy is huge. It can have a spiral, round, or egglike shape, or have no specific shape at all.

____

Name ______________________________

4. Focus Skill Main Idea and Details

Use this space to complete the graphic organizer shown in the Reading Review of the Student Edition.

Write two supporting details for each main idea about stars.

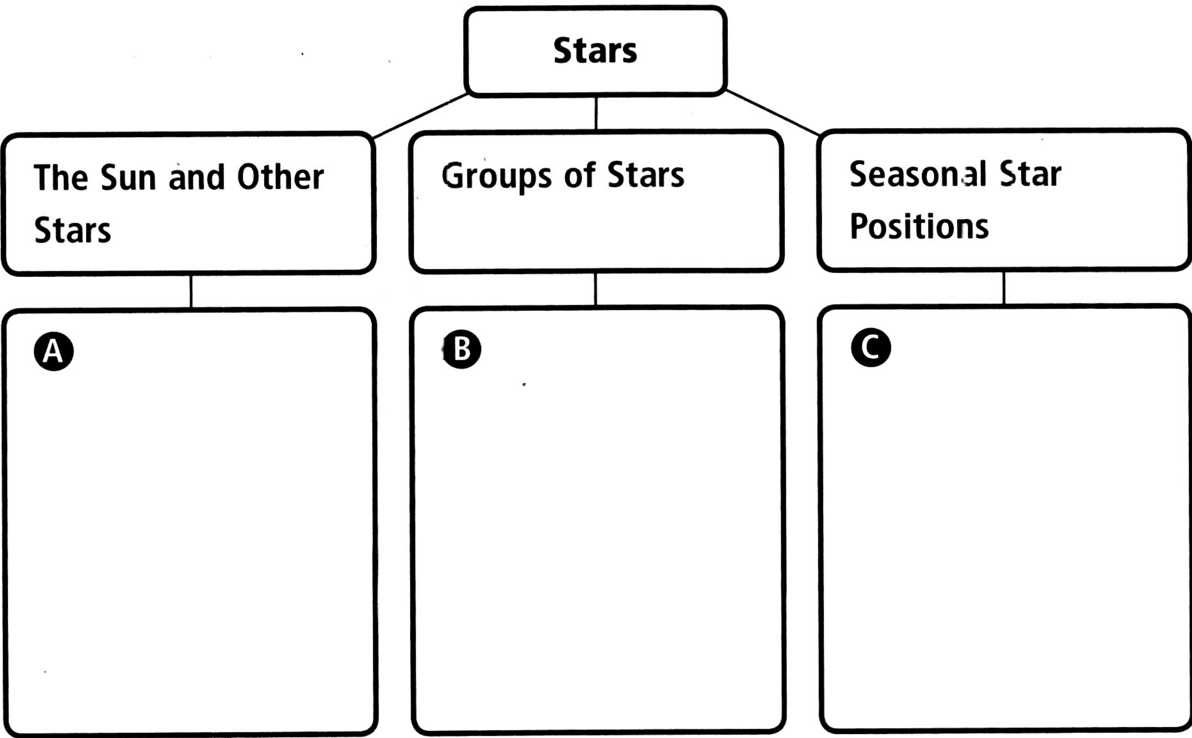

5. Critical Thinking and Problem Solving

Explain why the night sky would appear different to someone who lives in the Northern Hemisphere than to someone who lives in the Southern Hemisphere.

____

____

____

____

Name ______________________________

Date ______________________________

Write a Story About the Future

Narrative Writing–Story

Write a story about one day in the future. Imagine that your main character's community runs on solar energy alone. Describe homes, transportation, and communications powered by the sun. Be imaginative, and use descriptive language. Use the story map to help you plan your writing.

Character:	Setting (Name of future solar community):
How does the day begin?	
How does the character travel?	
What do home appliances look like?	
How does the day end?	

Name ______________________

Date ______________________

Vocabulary Power

Matter and Its Properties

A. Analogy

An analogy is made of two pairs of words. The words in each pair are related to each other in the same way. Think about the relationships in the following pairs of words. Then choose a word from the box to complete the analogy.

gas	liquid	mass	volume

1. *Temperature* is to *heat* as *sound* is to ______________.

2. *Height* is to *peak* as *weight* is to ______________.

3. *Meat* is to *food* as *oxygen* is to ______________.

4. *Cotton* is to *fabric* as *water* is to ______________.

B. Context Clues

Write the word from the box that best answers the following questions.

suspension	solubility	density	solution

5. Which word describes the amount of matter in an object compared to the space it takes up?

   ____

6. Which word describes a mixture in which different types of matter are mixed evenly with each other?

   ____

Name ____________________

Date ____________________

Lesson Quick Study

Lesson 1 - How Can Physical Properties Be Used to Identify Matter?

1. **Inquiry Skills Practice–Display Data**

Observe the physical properties of a book, a penny, and a cotton ball. Use the chart to display your observations.

Object	How It Looks	How It Feels
book		
penny		
cotton ball		

2. **Use Vocabulary**

Match the clue on the left to the term on the right.

____ The amount of matter in an object compared to the space it takes up — **A.** matter

____ The amount of space matter takes up — **B.** mass

____ Anything that takes up space — **C.** volume

____ The amount of matter something contains — **D.** density

3. Focus Skill **Reading Skill Practice–Main Idea and Details**

Read the selection. Underline the main idea. List at least 2 details about the main idea.

So that food is tasty and fresh, chefs need to know its physical properties. For example, chefs look at fruit and vegetables to be sure they are fresh and not rotten. They feel lettuce to be sure it is crisp, not limp. Chefs taste the food to see if salt needs to be added. What would food taste like without knowing its properties?

____

____

Name ______________________________

4. **Focus Skill** **Main Idea and Details**

Complete this graphic organizer.

Main Idea: Ⓐ ______________ **is the relationship between mass and volume.**

Two objects with high density:

Ⓑ ______________________________

Ⓒ ______________________________

Two objects with low density:

Ⓓ ______________________________

Ⓔ ______________________________

5. **Critical Thinking and Problem Solving**

Suppose you are helping a friend move. You lift a small box and notice that it is very heavy. You then lift a large box and notice that is very light. From what you have learned about density, how can you explain the differences?

____

____

____

____

Name ______________________________

Date ______________________________

Lesson Quick Study

Lesson 2 - How Does Matter Change States?

1. **Inquiry Skill Practice–Infer**

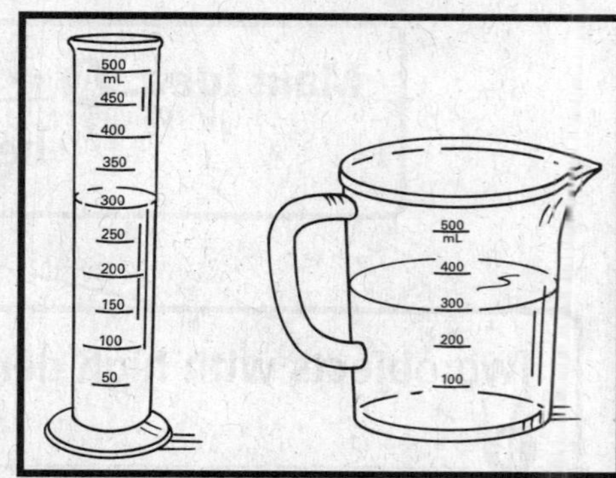

Millen poured 300 mL of water into each container. Each has the same amount of water. Why does one look fuller than the other?

____

____

____

____

2. **Use Vocabulary**

Write a complete sentence that uses the words *state of matter* correctly.

____

____

3. Focus Skill **Reading Skill Practice–Cause and Effect**

Read the selection. Describe the Cause and Effect of changing states of matter.

Long ago, an engineer named James Watt helped improve the steam engine. His engine burned wood or coal to heat water. The water traveled through pipes that led to a water tank. The heated water turned into steam. The expanding steam pushed on a metal piston. The back-and-forth motion of the piston caused the engine's wheels to turn.

____

____

Name ______________________________

4. Focus Skill **Cause and Effect**

Complete the graphic organizer.

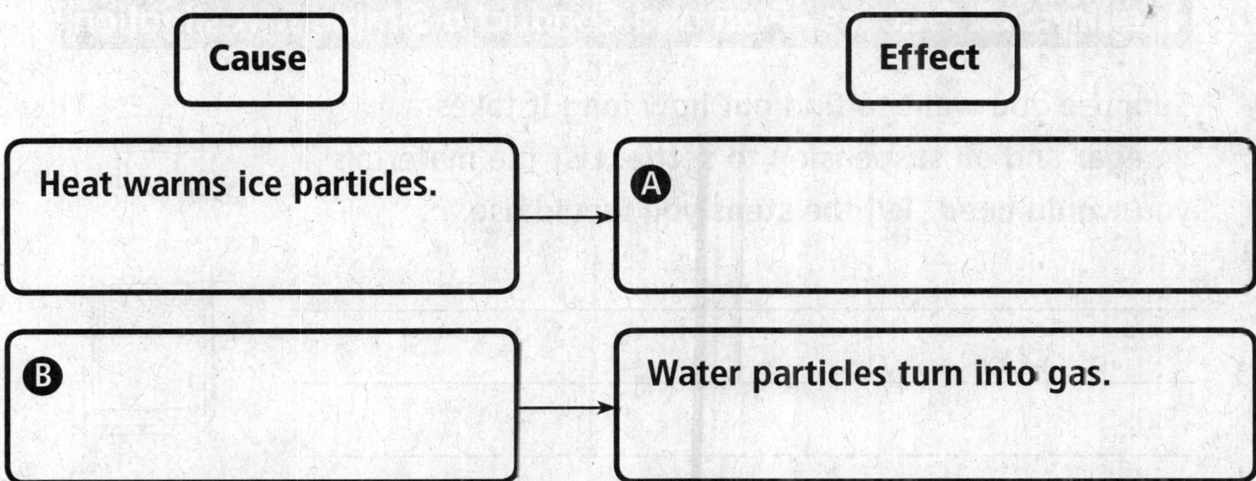

5. **Critical Thinking and Problem Solving**

Suppose an adult is cooking and a plastic cooking spoon gets too close to the hot stove. As soon as he notices, he takes the spoon away from the heat. The shape of the spoon has already changed slightly. How can you explain the change?

____

____

Name ______________________________

Date ______________________________

Lesson 3 - What Are Mixtures and Solutions?

1. Inquiry Skill Practice–Plan and Conduct a Simple Investigation

Suppose you want to find out how long it takes a vinegar and oil suspension to settle. List the materials you would need. Tell the steps you would use.

____

____

____

2. Use Vocabulary

Complete each sentence with the correct term from the box.

mixture
solution
suspension

A ________________ is different kinds of matter mixed completely.

A ________________ is two or more substances combined without changing any of them.

________________ is when matter is not spread out evenly in a mixture. Some matter settles to the bottom.

3. Focus Skill Reading Skill Practice–Main Idea and Details

Read the selection. Underline the main idea. List at least 2 details.

Different tools are used to help learn about blood, which is a mixture. One tool is a centrifuge. A centrifuge is used in labs to divide blood into its parts. Another tool is a microscope. The microsope lets scientists see the tiny parts that make up blood.

____

____

Name ______________________________

4. **Focus Skill** **Main Idea and Details**

Complete the graphic organizer. List two details about each main idea.

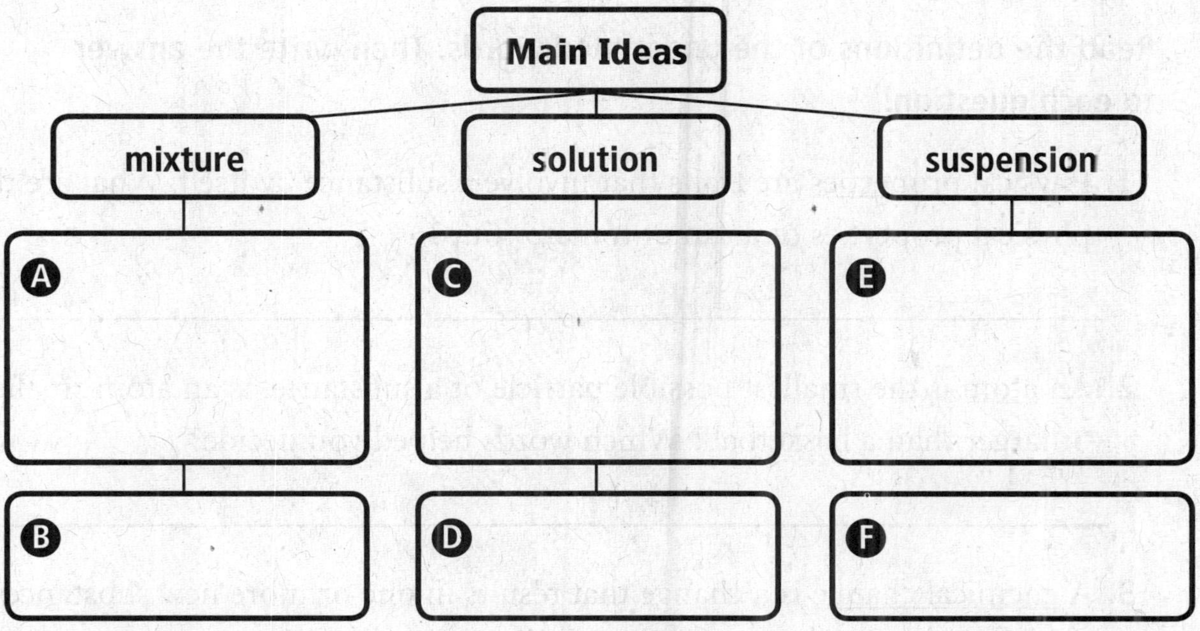

5. **Critical Thinking and Problem Solving**

Suppose you have two glasses of water. You pour a spoonful of baking soda into the first. You pour a spoonful of dirt into the second. You stir each for one minute. What do you predict will happen? How can you decide if each mixture is a solution or a suspension?

____

____

____

____

Name ______________________

Date ______________________

Vocabulary Power

Changes in Matter

A. Explore Word Meanings

Read the definitions of the underlined words. Then write the answer to each question.

1. Physical properties are traits that involve a substance by itself. What are the physical properties of a can of tomato soup?

____

2. An atom is the smallest possible particle of a substance. Is an atom smaller or larger than a basketball? Which words helped you decide?

____

3. A chemical change is a change that results in one or more new substances. What chemical change is likely to occur when a metal chair is left outside in the air and rain?

____

B. Multiple-Meaning Words

Read each sentence and the definitions of the underlined word. Circle the letter that shows which way the word has been used.

4. Water is a compound made up of hydrogen and oxygen.

A. two or more different elements that have chemically combined

B. a word made up of two smaller words

5. All of the clothes and shoes in my closet are examples of matter.

A. the meaning of something

B. anything that has mass and takes up space

Name ______________________

Date ______________________

Lesson 1 - What Is Matter Made Of?

1. Inquiry Skill Practice–Draw Conclusions

Suppose you have a large box that has some deflated balloons. What will happen if you inflate all the balloons, and put them back in the box? Why will this happen?

____

____

2. Use Vocabulary

Write a complete sentence that uses the term(s) correctly.

matter: ______________________________________

atom, element: ________________________________

3. Focus Skill Reading Skill Practice–Main Idea and Details

Read the selection. Underline the main idea. List at least 2 details.

An element is a substance that is made up of only one type of atom. Elements can be classified into groups. Among the different kinds of groups of elements are the metals and the nonmetals. Although not all metals are elements, scientists still classified elements as metals because a vast majority of them fit into this category. Examples of the elements in the metal group are gold and silver. One example of the element in the nonmetal group is sulfur.

____

____

____

Name ______________________________

4. **Main Idea and Details**

Complete this graphic organizer.

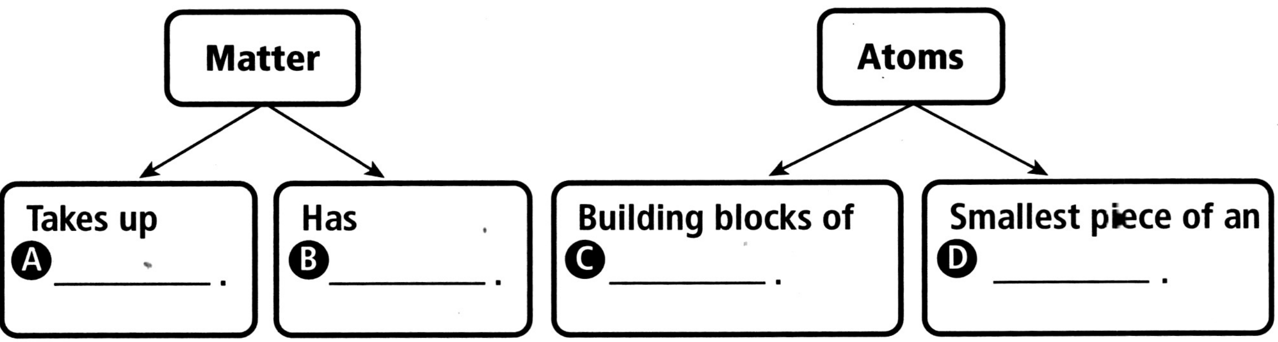

5. **Critical Thinking and Problem Solving**

Suppose you are an electrician. Will you use a metal or nonmetal element to install wiring? Explain your answer.

____

____

____

Name ______________________________

Date ______________________________

Lesson 2 - What Are Physical Changes in Matter?

1. Inquiry Skills Practice–Make a Hypothesis

The ice prism on the left and the ice on the right were made with exactly the same amount of water. Why does one seem to have more? How can you show that both were made with the same amount of water?

____

____

2. Use Vocabulary

Complete each sentence with the correct term from the box.

change of state
physical change

A ____________________ is when a substance melts, freezes, boils, or condenses.

A ____________________ happens when a substance changes its appearance but not its composition.

3. Focus Skill Reading Skill Practice–Compare and Contrast

Read the selection. Compare and contrast the three states of water.

Mrs. Robins boils a pot of water for the spaghetti. Mr. Robins puts ice cubes into the pitcher. The children pour water into the pitcher. It is almost dinner time.

____

____

Name ______________________________

4. **Compare and Contrast**

Complete the graphic organizer.

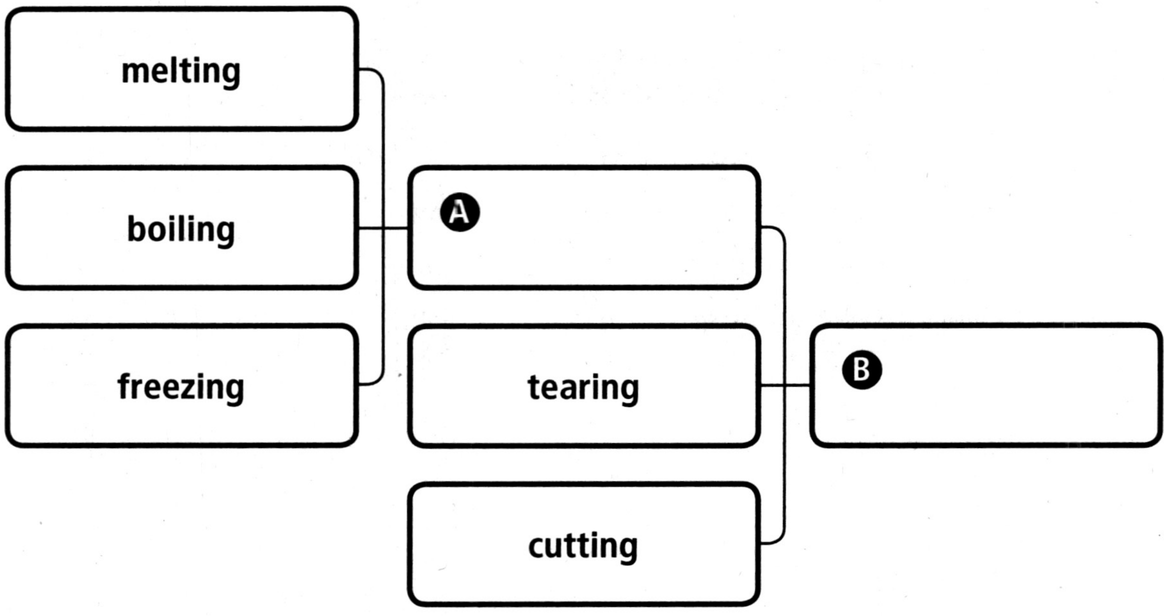

5. **Critical Thinking and Problem Solving**

Suppose you are given two containers of clear liquid. You know that one contains water and the other contains salt and water mixed together. But your friend thinks they are both water because they both look the same. How can you prove to your friend that one container has salt water in it, without tasting the liquids?

____

____

____

Name ______________________________

Date ______________________________

Lesson 3 - How Does Matter React Chemically?

1. Inquiry Skill Practice–Draw Conclusions

Look at the table. What conclusion can you draw about how substances affect pennies?

____

____

Substance	Reaction
acetic acid [vinegar]	Penny turned green.
water	Penny remained the same.
citric acid [lemon juice]	Penny turned green.

2. Use Vocabulary

Match the clue on the left to the term on the right.

____ Water is made of two elements.

____ Water is colorless and odorless.

____ Another term for chemical change

A. physical properties

B. chemical reaction

C. compound

3. Focus Skill Reading Skill Practice–Compare and Contrast

Read the selection. Compare and contrast elements and compounds.

An element is made up of only one kind of atom. For instance, hydrogen is an element. All of the atoms that make up hydrogen are the same. A compound is made up of more than one kind of atom. Baking soda is a compound.

____

____

____

Name ______________________________

4. Focus Skill **Compare and Contrast**

Copy and complete the graphic organizer.

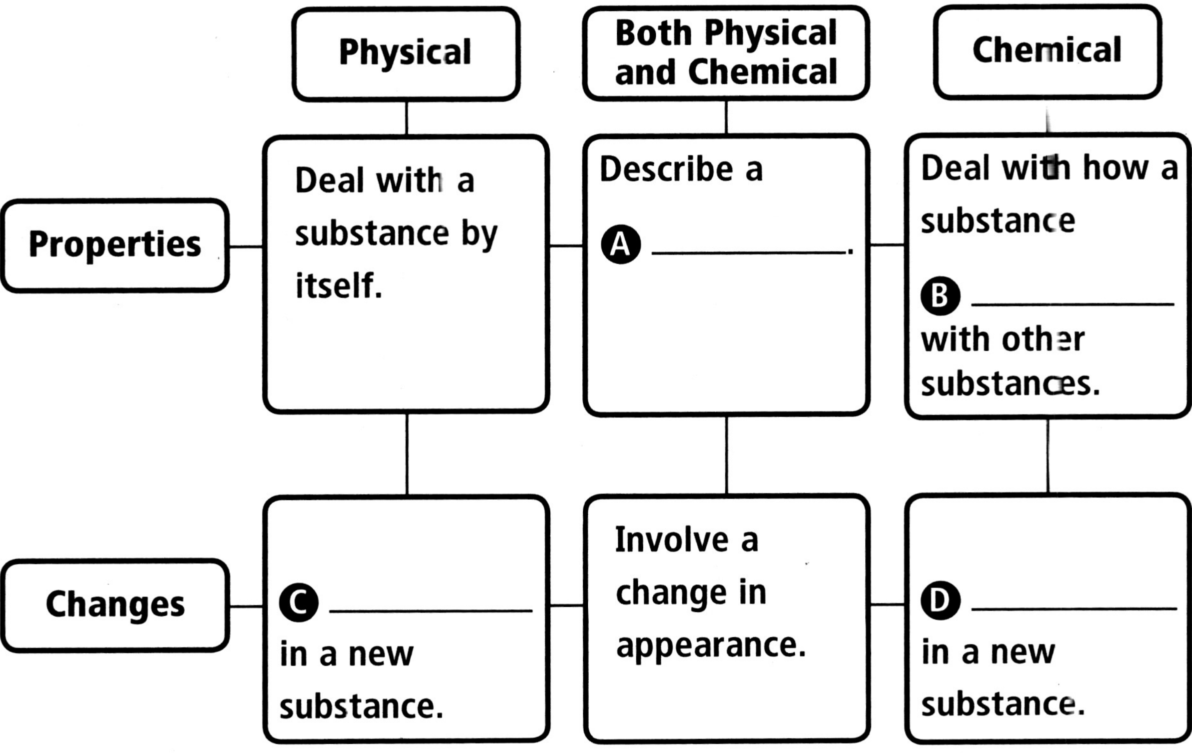

5. **Critical Thinking and Problem Solving**

Leaves change their color in autumn. Is this process a physical change or a chemical change? Explain your reasoning.

____

____

____

Name ______________________

Date ______________________

Vocabulary Power

Sound

A. Prefixes and Latin Roots

Read the table of prefixes and Latin root words. Then write a likely definition for each numbered word. You may go back to check and revise your definition when you have finished this chapter.

Prefix	Meaning	Latin Root	Meaning
ab–	away, down	*sorbere*	to drink in
re–	back	*flectere*	to bend
trans–	over, across	*mittere*	to send

1. reflection ______________________
2. absorption ______________________
3. transmission ______________________

B. Related Words

Read each word in the box. Find the group of words to which it is related in meaning or structure. Write the word on the line.

intensity	vibration	frequency

4. swing, vibrate, quiver ______________________
5. infrequent, frequently, frequented ______________________
6. strength, power, intent ______________________

Name ______________________________

Date ______________________________

Lesson 1 - What Is Sound?

1. Inquiry Skill Practice–Hypothesize

Rob's mom is vacuuming. Rob comes into the room and talks to her. She does not hear him. Form a hypothesis to explain why she cannot hear Rob.

____

____

2. Use Vocabulary

Complete each sentence with the correct term from the box.

vibration
pitch
intensity

The ________________ of his voice is higher when he screams.

________________ was felt during the earthquake.

The ________________ of a motorcycle's sound is very large because it produces high-energy sound waves.

3. Focus Skill Reading Skill Practice–Main Idea and Details

Read the selection. Underline the main idea. List at least 2 details.

Sound is produced by vibrating objects. Every time an object vibrates in air, it produces a sound. The sound could be low or high and loud or soft. The sound you hear depends on the vibration of the object. When you tip-toe, you make little vibrations on the floor. The sound you hear is soft. If you stomp, you make larger vibrations. The sound you hear is loud.

____

____

Name ______________________________

4. **Main Idea and Details**

Complete this graphic organizer.

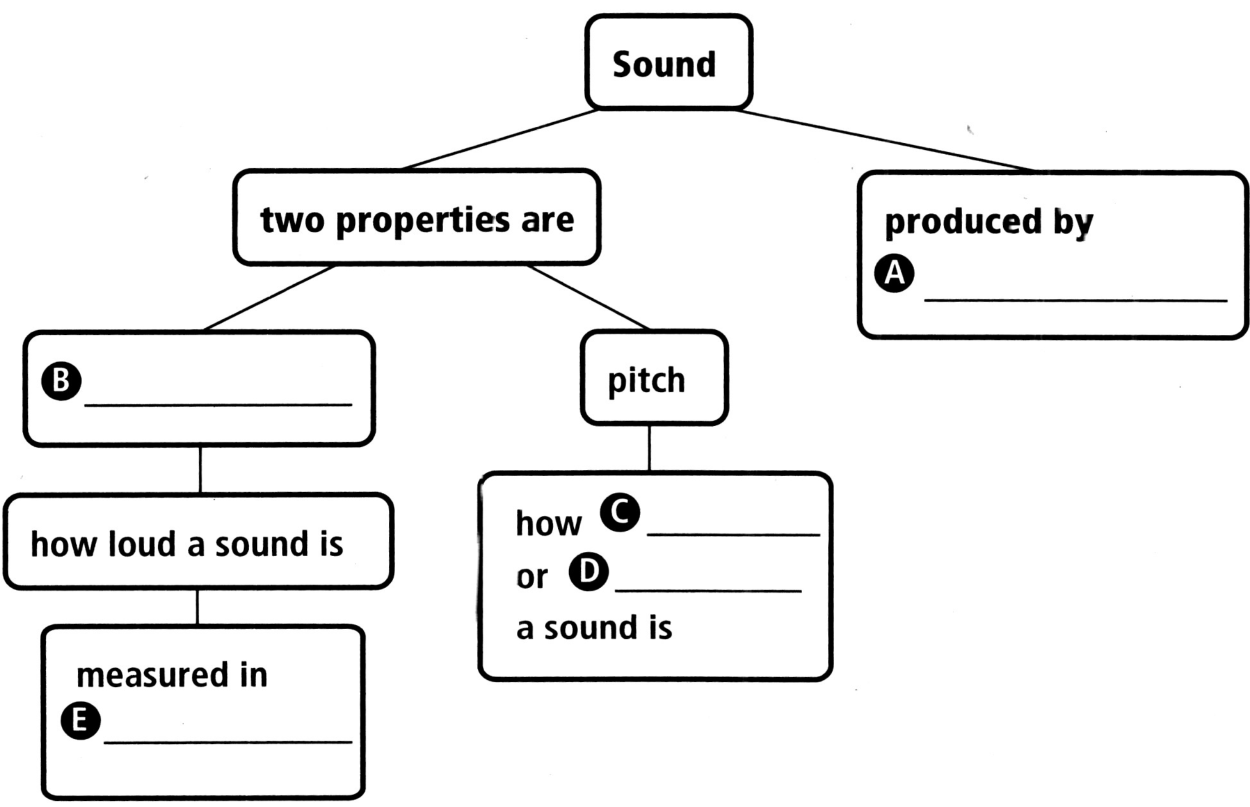

5. **Critical Thinking and Problem Solving**

Sometimes people listen to the railroad tracks to find out if a train is coming from far away. What do you suppose they can hear?

____

____

____

Name ______________________________

Date ______________________________

Lesson Quick Study

Lesson 2 - What Are the Properties of Waves?

1. **Inquiry Skill Practice–Use Numbers**

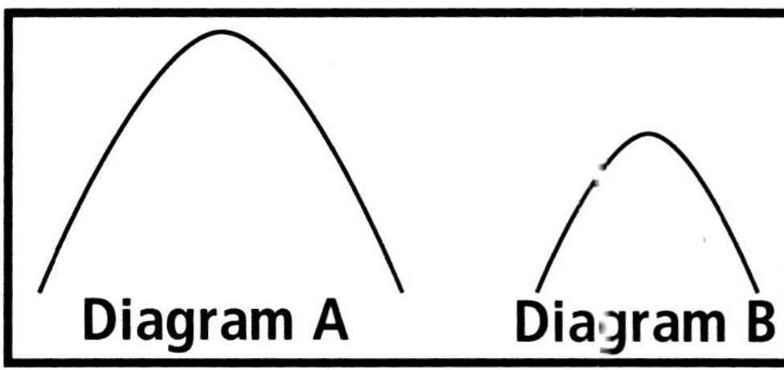

Look at the diagrams of the two sound waves to the right. How could you use numbers to describe them?

____

____

2. **Use Vocabulary**

Match the clue on the left to the term on the right.

____ A measure of how much energy a wave has — **A.** wavelength

____ The length of one wave — **B.** frequency

____ The number of waves that pass in a second — **C.** amplitude

3. Focus Skill **Reading Skill Practice–Main Idea and Details**

Read the selection. Underline the main idea. List at least 2 details.

Describing a sound wave is not like describing a pencil or a toy. You can not see sound waves. To describe sound waves, you use the terms *wavelength*, *frequency*, and *amplitude*. Sound waves are somewhat like water waves. The point from which a wave starts to where the next wave starts is its length, or *wavelength*. The number of waves that pass in one second is the *frequency*. The amplitude is the amount of energy a wave has.

____

____

Name ______________________________

4. Focus Skill Main Idea and Details

Copy and complete this graphic organizer.

Main Idea	There are two types of waves.	The properties of sound waves affect the sound you hear.	
Details	**A** __________ waves move across the direction of travel.	**B** __________ is the number of waves that pass by in a second.	Higher-frequency waves make a **D** __________-pitched sound.
	Longitudinal waves move back and forth along the direction of travel.	Amplitude measures the **C** __________ of a wave.	**E** __________ amplitude waves make a softer sound.

5. Critical Thinking and Problem Solving

Suppose you throw a tennis ball and a basketball against a wall. You throw each from the same distance and with the same force. The basketball sounds louder than the tennis ball. What can you infer about their amplitude and loudness?

____

____

Name ______________________________

Date ______________________________

Lesson Quick Study

Lesson 3 - How Do Sound Waves Travel?

1. Inquiry Skill Practice–Identify Variables

Jackie wanted to test how the echo of a large book differed in three rooms. The rooms are empty and the same size. The first has carpet, the second has tile, and the third has a wood floor. Finally she dropped the book in a room with tile floors. What variable did Jackie change?

____

2. Use Vocabulary

Write a complete sentence for each term that uses the term correctly.

reflection: ______________________________

absorption: ______________________________

transmission: ______________________________

3. Focus Skill Reading Skill Practice–Compare and Contrast

Read the selection. Compare and contrast recorded music and live music.

Recorded music and live music sound different. Mostly, recorded music is done in a soundproof studio. There, sound is absorbed by thick cushioned walls and carpet. Outside noises are not heard. At a concert, live music sounds reflect from many surfaces. There are no cushioned walls or thick carpeting that keep the noise from spreading.

____

____

____

Name ______________________________

4. **Compare and Contrast**

Complete the graphic organizer.

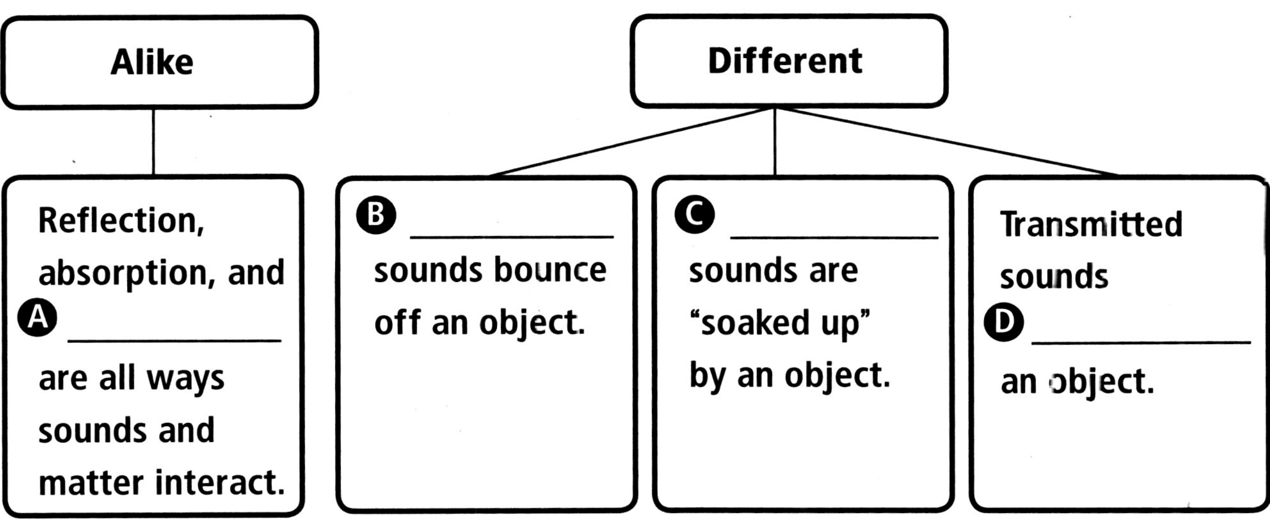

5. **Critical Thinking and Problem Solving**

How do you suppose a person could damage his or her hearing by listening to loud sounds, such as loud concerts, loud airplanes, or loud construction equipment?

____

____

Name ______________________

Date ______________________

Vocabulary Power

Light and Heat

A. Suffixes

Adding a suffix to a word changes its meaning and usage. The suffix *–tion* added to a verb changes a verb into a noun and means "the act of doing something." Read the words below and add the suffix *–tion.* Then write the definition of the new word.

1. reflect + tion ______________________
2. refract + tion ______________________
3. conduct + tion ______________________
4. convect + tion ______________________
5. radiate + tion ______________________

B. Explore Word Meanings

Use a glossary to find the meaning of the underlined words. Then write your answer to each question.

6. When the motor of your family's car is turned off, the radiator collects and removes waste heat from the engine. What is *waste heat*?

____

7. Solar heat is an example of energy transfer. What does *energy transfer* mean?

____

Name ______________________

Date ______________________

Lesson Quick Study

Lesson 1 - How Does Light Behave?

1. Inquiry Skill Practice–Communicate

Study both pictures. Communicate what happens in each picture.

____

____

____

____

2. Use Vocabulary

Match the clue on the left to the term on the right.

____ The bending of light **A.** light

____ A form of energy that can travel through space **B.** reflection

____ The bouncing of light off an object **C.** refraction

3. Focus Skill Reading Skill Practice–Cause and Effect

Read the selection. Describe a cause and effect related to light.

Linda buys two plants. She puts one of the plants in a large box made of glass. Linda puts the other plant in a box made of wood. She puts both boxes outside in the yard in the sun. Linda waters the plants. After a few days, Linda notices that the plant in the glass box is green and growing, and the plant in the wooden box is yellow and droopy.

____

____

Name ________________________________

4. Focus Skill **Cause and Effect**

Complete the graphic organizer.

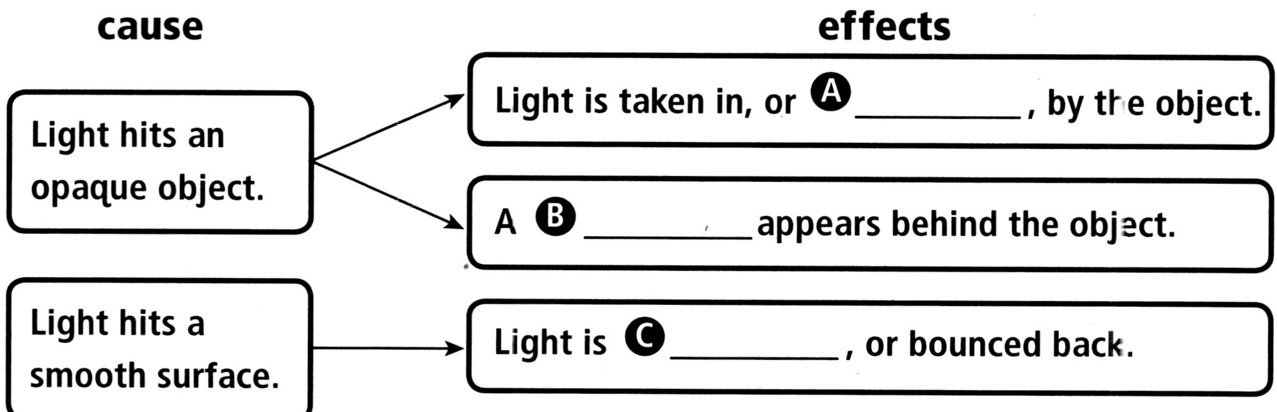

5. **Critical Thinking and Problem Solving**

In the picture on the left, Sam is standing in his backyard at noon. In the picture on the right, he is standing in his backyard at 5 p.m. Draw his shadows at each time of day. Explain your reasoning.

____

____

____

____

Name ______________________

Date ______________________

Lesson Quick Study

Lesson 2 - How Can Heat Be Transferred?

1. Inquiry Skill Practice–Predict

Radiation

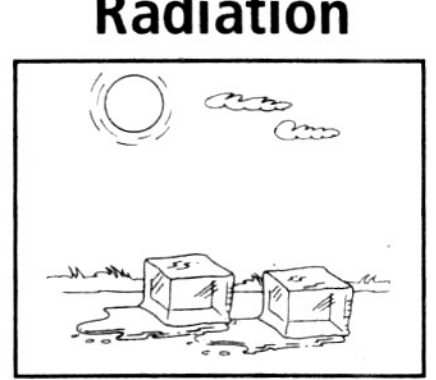

Conduction

Convection

Predict which method of heat transfer will melt the ice cubes fastest. Explain.

____

____

____

2. Use Vocabulary

Complete each sentence with the correct term from the box.

conduction convection radiation

The sun warms Earth through ______________.

______________ is when heat travels from one part of an object to another part of that object.

______________ is when heat moves from a warmer area to a cooler area in a gas or liquid.

3. Focus Skill — Reading Skill Practice–Main Idea and Details

Read the selection. Underline the main idea. List at least 3 details.

Maria uses heat to make pasta. First, she carefully puts the pot on the stove to boil water. Maria fills the pot with cold water and turns on the burner. The water starts to warm up, beginning at the bottom, where the water is closest to the pot. When the water boils, Maria puts the pasta in. Once the pasta is done, she will use thick pot holders to take the pot from the stove.

____

____

Name ______________________________

4. **Focus Skill** **Main Idea and Details**

Complete this graphic organizer.

Main Idea: Heat is the Ⓐ ____________________ of thermal energy.

Heat moves through solids by Ⓑ __________.	Heat moves through liquids by Ⓒ __________.	Heat moves through gases by Ⓓ __________.	Heat moves through space by Ⓔ __________.

5. **Critical Thinking and Problem Solving**

Craig measured the temperature of air in two different places. One of the readings suggested that the particles in the air were moving slowly, on average. The other reading suggested that the particles in the air were moving very fast, on average. What exactly does this tell you about the temperatures in each place?

____

____

____

____

Name ______________________________

Date ______________________________

Lesson Quick Study

Lesson 3 - How is Heat Produced and Used?

1. **Inquiry Skill Practice–Interpret Data**

Look at the graph. Why do you think the temperature changed over time?

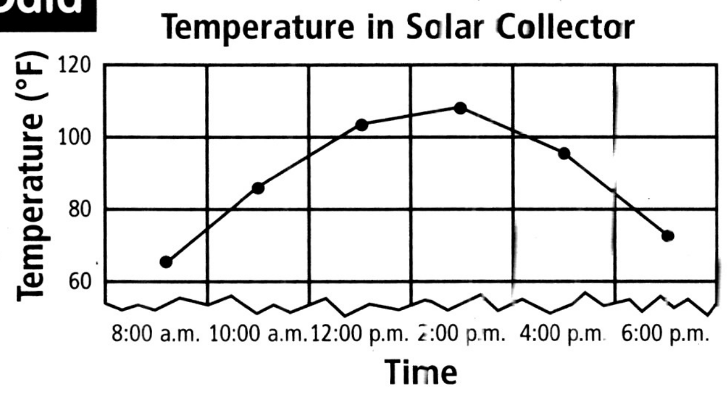

____

____

Temperature in Solar Collector

2. **Use Vocabulary**

Write a complete sentence that uses the term correctly.

energy transfer: ______________________________

waste heat: ______________________________

3. Focus Skill **Reading Skill Practice–Main Idea and Details**

Read the selection. Underline the main idea. List at least 2 details.

A hot water bottle is used to transfer heat to sore muscles. Hot water bottles are made of thick, strong rubber with a firm screw-on cap. A hot water bottle works by filling it with very warm water and placing it on the area that needs heat. After several hours, the bottle will feel cold to the touch.

____

____

Name ______________________________

4. Focus Skill Main Idea and Details

Use this space to complete the graphic organizer shown in Reading Review of the Student Edition.

Copy and complete the graphic organizer.

Main Idea: Heat comes from many sources.

Heat from the (A) ____________ travels through space to Earth.	Burning (B) ____________ produces heat.	Wires give off heat when (C) ____________ flows through them.

5. Critical Thinking and Problem Solving

Suppose you are in the yard playing out in the sun. You feel hot. How do you think you will release this waste heat from your body to allow it to cool off?

____

____

____

____

Name ______________________________

Date ______________________________

Write About Simple Machines

Persuasive Argument–Composition

Suppose that you have a friend who thinks simple machines are no longer useful today. On a separate piece of paper, write a four-paragraph composition in which you try to convince your friend that simple machines are important in everyday life. Your composition should have an introduction stating your argument, two paragraphs supporting your main point, and a brief conclusion. Use the web diagram below to organize your ideas before you begin writing.

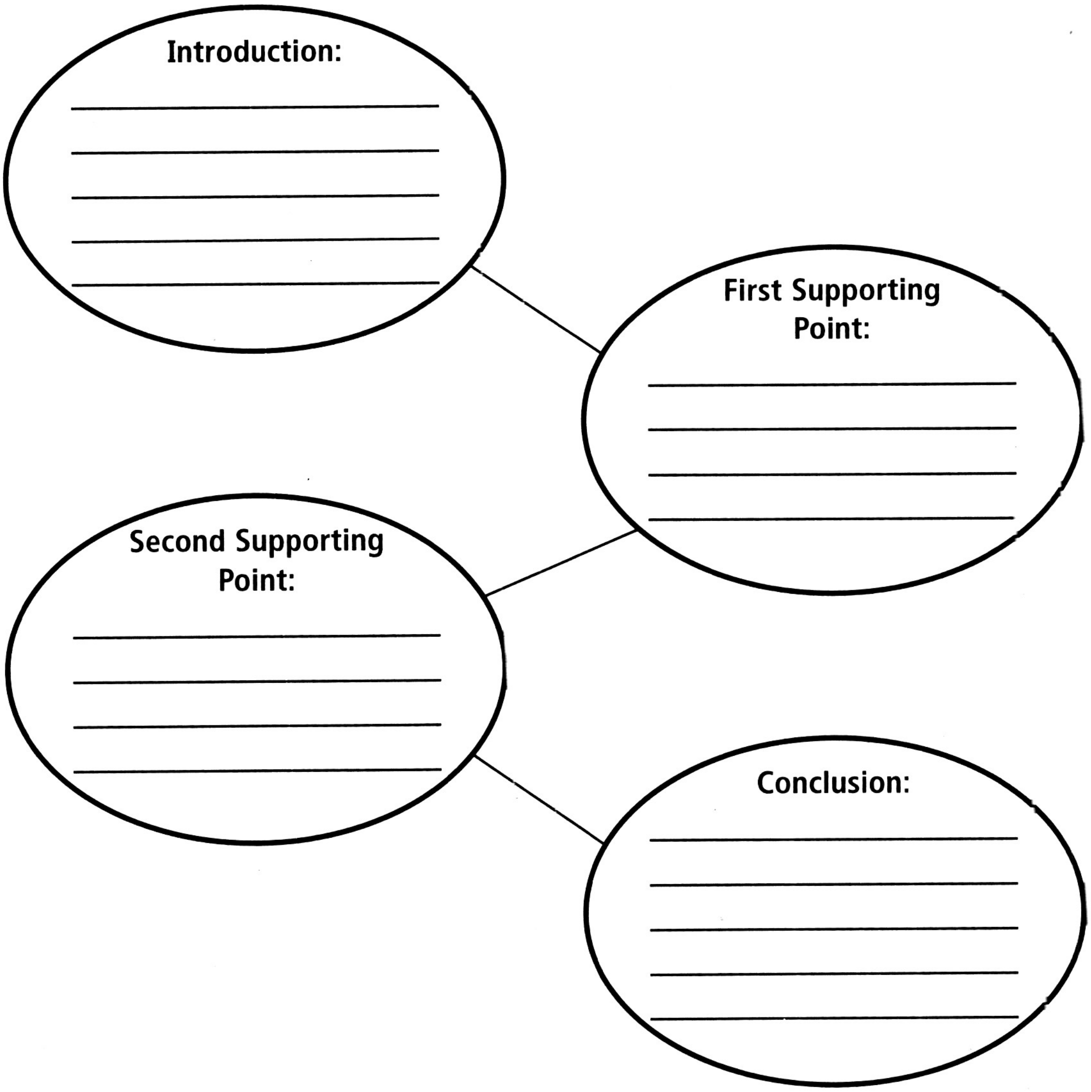

Introduction:

____
____
____
____
____

First Supporting Point:

____
____
____
____

Second Supporting Point:

____
____
____
____

Conclusion:

____
____
____
____
____

Name ______________________

Date ______________________

Vocabulary Power

Making and Using Electricity

A. Analogies

An analogy is made of two pairs of words. The words in each pair are related to each other in the same way. Think about the relationships in the following pairs of words. Then choose a word from the box to complete the analogy.

conductor	generator	insulator	magnet

1. *Orbit* is to *moon* as *attract* is to ______________.

2. *Solar energy* is to *sun* as *electricity* is to ______________.

3. *Stove* is to *appliance* as *metal* is to ______________.

4. *Banana* is to *skin* as *wires* is to ______________.

B. Classify/Categorize

Read the words in each list below. Label the category to which each group of words belongs.

5. potential energy, kinetic energy, chemical energy, mechanical energy

____

6. static electricity, current electricity

____

7. solar energy, geothermal energy

____

8. series circuit, parallel circuit

____

Name ____________________

Date ____________________

Lesson 1 - What Is Electricity?

1. **Inquiry Skill Practice–Record Data**

Suppose you are testing how the number of batteries affects bulb brightness. What heads would you use on this data table?

2. **Use Vocabulary**

Match the clue on the left to the correct term on the right.

____ electricity flows in only one path	**A.** static electricity
____ lets electricity flow through easily	**B.** current electricity
____ electrical charge that builds up in an object	**C.** series circuit
____ electricity can flow in more than one path	**D.** parallel circuit
____ a steady stream of electricity	**E.** conductor
____ does not carry electricity easily	**F.** insulator

3. Focus Skill **Reading Skill Practice–Sequence**

Put the following events about lightning in the correct sequence. Number the steps 1 to 5.

____ The ice crystals gain negative charges.

____ Lightning is seen.

____ Ice crystals in a thunder cloud rub together.

____ The ground loses negative charges, so it is left with a positive charge.

____ Negative charges move from the clouds to the ground.

Name ______________________

4. Focus Skill **Sequence**

Complete the graphic organizer. Use the terms shown in the box to describe a working series circuit.

bulb
more wire
switch
battery or wall outlet
wire

5. **Critical Thinking and Problem Solving**

Suppose you have one electrical wire with many lights. One of the bulbs breaks. The entire strand of lights goes out. What caused this to happen? Explain your reasoning.

____

____

____

Name ______________________

Date ______________________

Lesson 2 - How Are Electricity and Magnetism Related?

1. **Inquiry Skill Practice–Compare**

Marvin has two magnets. He put two large paper clips at the end of his desk. Marvin put one magnet at about 9 inches away from the paper clips. He put the second magnet at about 12 inches away from the paper clips. He noticed that both paper clips reached the magnets at the same time. Why do you suppose this happened?

____

____

2. **Use Vocabulary**

Complete each sentence with the correct term from the box.

magnetic field electromagnet electric motor

The space around a magnet where the force of the magnet acts is a ______________.

A temporary magnet is an ______________.

The fan has an ______________ that changes electric energy to mechanical energy.

3. Focus Skill **Reading Skill Practice–Compare and Contrast**

Read the selection. Compare and contrast magnetic poles.

Magnets have two poles. They are the south-seeking pole and the north-seeking pole. These poles are where a magnet exerts the strongest force. Opposite poles attract. If you place an S and an N pole

(cont'd.)

Name ______________________________

near each other, they pull together. Like poles repel. If you place two N or two S poles together, they push apart.

____

____

4. Focus Skill **Compare and Contrast**

Complete this graphic organizer to compare and contrast electricity and magnetism.

Alike	Different
Opposite types **A** ____________ .	Magnetic **B** ____________ interact.
Like types repel.	Electric charges interact.
	Moving magnets make **C** ____________ ____________ .
	Moving charges make an electromagnet.

5. **Critical Thinking and Problem Solving**

Ana noticed that a strong bar magnet she was playing with attracted a small plastic car. She could use the magnet to move the car around on the floor. What do you think caused the magnet to move the plastic car? Explain your reasoning.

____

____

____

____

Name ______________________

Date ______________________

Lesson Quick Study

Lesson 3 - What Are Some Sources of Electricity?

1. Inquiry Skill Practice–Identify Variables

Suppose a scientist wants to find out which form of energy works better in a model car. She wants to test gasoline, hydrogen fuel, and electricity. She will use the same car for each test. The tests will be performed on the same road. What variables changed?

____

2. Use Vocabulary

Match the clue on the left to the correct term on the right.

____ the energy of sunlight	**A.** potential energy
____ energy of position	**B.** kinetic energy
____ energy of motion	**C.** geothermal energy
____ heat from inside Earth	**D.** solar energy

3. Focus Skill Reading Skill Practice–Main Idea and Details

Read the selection. Underline the main idea. List at least 3 details.

We acquire energy from different sources. Energy can be obtained from hydroelectric power. Hydroelectric power is the energy from falling water. Another source of energy is geothermal energy. It is obtained from deep inside Earth. Solar energy can also be used as a source of energy. It is obtained from the sun.

____

____

Name ______________________________

4. Focus Skill **Main Idea and Details**

Complete the graphic organizers.

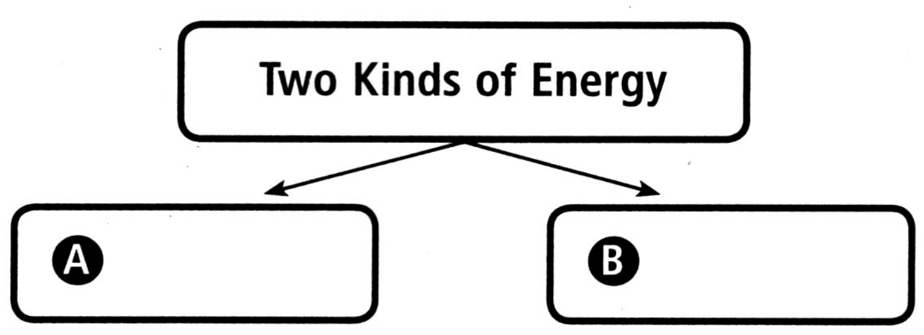

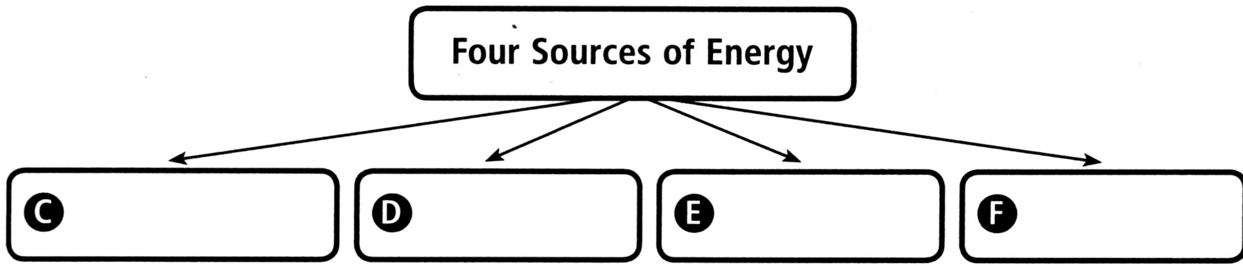

5. **Critical Thinking and Problem Solving**

Marcos builds two ramps. One ramp is steeper than the other. He puts a tennis ball at the top of each ramp. Which tennis ball reached the bottom of the ramp faster? Which ball do you think had more kinetic energy? Explain.

____

____

____

____

____

Name ______________________

Date ______________________

Lesson Quick Study

Lesson 4 - How Do People Use Energy Resources?

1. **Inquiry Skill Practice–Classify**

Electricity is used at home, at school, and in our neighborhoods. Use the boxes below to write three ways we use electricity in each place.

At Home	At School	In Our Neighborhood

2. **Use Vocabulary**

Write a complete sentence that uses the term correctly.

chemical energy: ______________________

mechanical energy: ______________________

3. 

Reading Skill Practice–Main Idea and Details

Read the selection. Underline the main idea. List at least 2 details.

Mercy practices ways to save energy. She replaced all the bulbs that waste a lot of energy with energy-efficient bulbs. When Mercy passes by a room that is empty and the lights are on, she turns them off. She also turns off the television when no one is watching it. Mercy knows that saving energy saves money.

____

____

Name ______________________________

4. Focus Skill **Main Idea and Details**

Complete this graphic organizer.

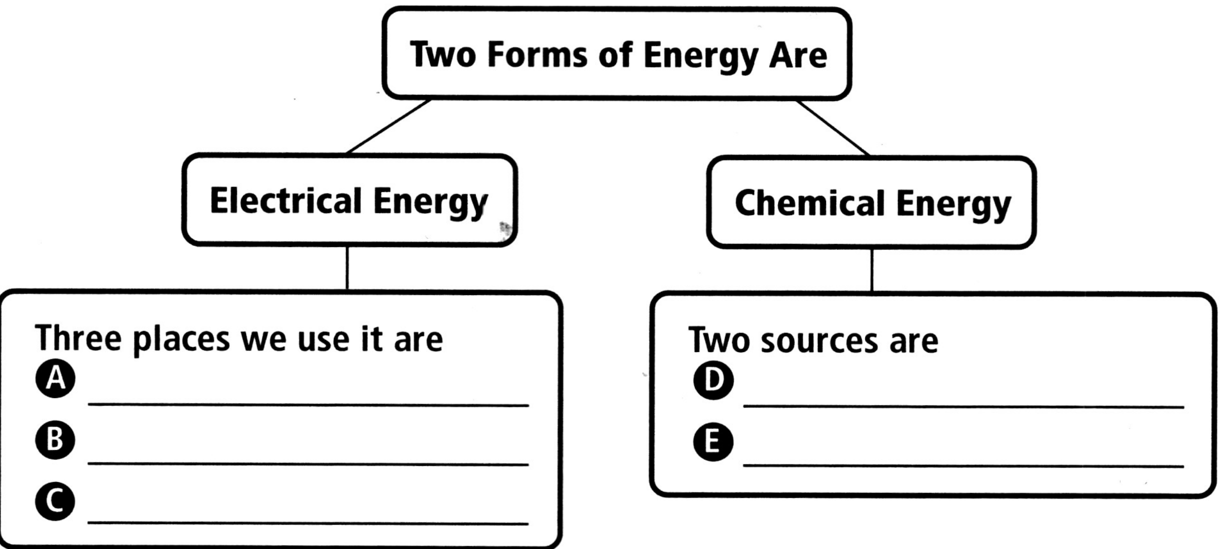

5. **Critical Thinking and Problem Solving**

The Smith family uses more energy during the summer than they do during the winter. What is a good explanation for this?

____

____

____

____

____

Name ______________________

Date ______________________

Vocabulary Power

Forces and Motion

A. Context Cues

Read each sentence below. Use context clues to figure out the meaning of each underlined word. Circle the letter of the correct meaning.

1. The driver slowed the car's acceleration as she drove down a steep slope.

   A. gas mileage
   B. temperature gauge
   C. a change in speed or direction
   D. a measure of pressure

2. The drill bit became hot from the friction created between the metal and the wood.

   A. sharp blade
   B. wood grain
   C. downward force
   D. resistance between two touching objects

3. The baseball's velocity was 90 miles per hour, north.

   A. an object's speed and direction
   B. an object's covering
   C. an object's size
   D. an object's degree of hardness

4. The inertia of the huge rock was so great that it took an enormous push to start it rolling downhill.

   A. speed of motion
   B. the tendency to stay at rest
   C. color
   D. tendency to float in water

5. People who parachute out of airplanes know that the force of gravity will bring them to the ground.

   A. the force that causes something to remain still
   B. the force that increases the speed of an object
   C. how something changes position
   D. the force that pulls objects toward Earth

Name ____________________
Date ____________________

Lesson Quick Study

Lesson 1 - How Is Motion Described and Measured?

1. **Inquiry Skill Practice–Communicate**

Betty walks to school from home. She starts by walking two blocks straight up from her house. Then she turns left and continues walking one block. At the end of the block, Betty makes two rights. The school is at the corner of that block. Make a drawing of Betty's path. How would you give directions from school to her house if she does not change her route?

____

____

2. **Use Vocabulary**

Match the clue on the left to the term on the right.

____ How a position changes during a unit of time	**A.** position
____ The location of an object	**B.** motion
____ The change of position of an object	**C.** speed

3. Focus Skill **Reading Skill Practice–Compare and Contrast**

Read the selection. Compare and Contrast the different runners.

Athletes know that running improves the strength of their heart and lungs. However, not all runners run the same way. Some runners are sprinters. They are good at racing quickly for short distances. Others are distance runners. They run at a slower speed but for a longer distance. Usually, distance racers would not perform well in a sprint because their muscles are not trained to let them start out

(cont'd.)

Name ______________________________

fast and continue to run fast. Sprinters become exhausted when they try to run a long distance.

____

____

____

4. Focus Skill **Compare and Contrast**

Complete this graphic organizer to compare and contrast a driver in a car passing a person who is walking on a sidewalk.

Alike	Different
Both are examples of (A) ________________.	The car has a greater (B) ________________ than the walker.
Both changes in position are compared to a (C) ________________.	The driver is (D) ________________ compared to the car seat but is (E) ________________ compared to the sidewalk.

5. **Critical Thinking and Problem Solving**

Suppose a cyclist takes 4 hours to reach the end of the race. He rides his bike 60 kilometers. What was the cyclist's speed? How do you know?

____

____

Name ______________________

Date ______________________

Lesson Quick Study

Lesson 2 - What Is Acceleration?

1. **Inquiry Skill Practice–Measure**

Below are pictures of forces. Use arrows to show the forces the students are exerting in each picture. The length of the arrows should indicate the sizes of the forces. Include a scale key.

2. **Use Vocabulary**

Write a complete sentence for each term in the box. Use the terms correctly.

velocity	force
acceleration	inertia

____

____

____

____

3. Focus Skill **Reading Skill Practice–Cause and Effect**

Read the selection. Describe a cause and its effect.

Danny pushed an empty cart into the library. It was easy for Danny to push the cart. He filled the cart with books. Danny tried pushing the cart out of the room, but he could barely move it. The cart was too

(cont'd.)

Name ______________________________

heavy to move easily. Danny realized that objects that have little mass are easier to move than objects that have a lot of mass.

____

____

4. Focus Skill **Cause and Effect**

Complete this graphic organizer.

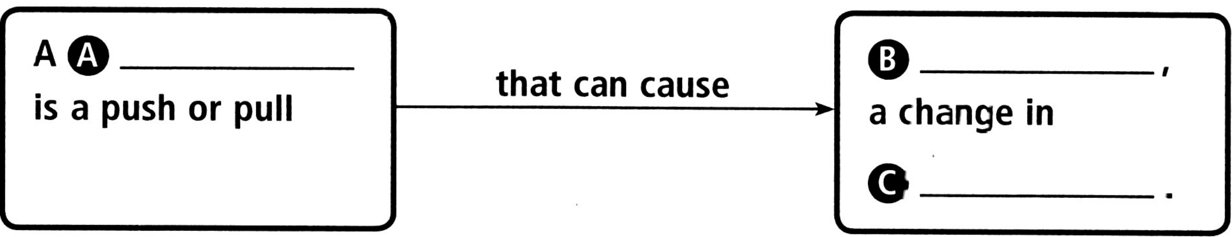

5. **Critical Thinking and Problem Solving**

Suppose a car is traveling north at 100 kilometers per hour. Another car is traveling in the opposite direction at the same speed. Are their velocities the same? Explain.

____

____

____

Name ______________________

Date ______________________

Lesson Quick Study

Lesson 3 - Why Is the Force of Gravity Important?

1. Inquiry Skill Practice–Experiment

Suppose you have a box. Describe an experiment to test how it slides across the different surfaces listed in the box. Circle the surface that you predict will cause the least friction.

rug
wooden floor
plastic with spikes (carpet protector)

____

____

2. Use Vocabulary

Complete each sentence with the correct term from the box.

gravity
gravitational
weight
friction

The ______________ force between Earth and the moon keeps the moon in orbit.

The ______________ caused by a rubber door stopper makes it difficult to open a door.

______________ is what helps us keep our feet on the ground.

The doctor asked the child to step on the scale to measure his ______________.

3. Focus Skill Reading Skill Practice–Main Idea and Details

Read the selection. Underline the main idea. List at least 2 details.

In this lesson, you learned about gravity. You learned that gravity is the force that pulls you towards Earth. Because of gravity you do not

(cont'd.)

Name ______________________

float in the air. Instead, you walk with your feet touching the ground. Gravity makes it possible to keep your books and pencils on your desk.

____

____

4. **Main Idea and Details**

Complete the graphic organizer.

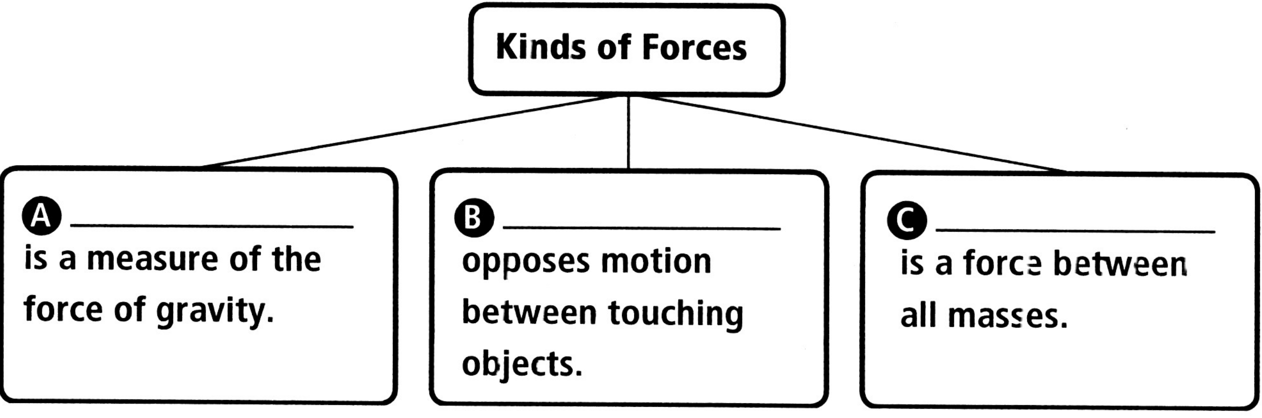

5. **Critical Thinking and Problem Solving**

Suppose Olga is traveling to a planet that has gravity half as strong as Earth's. How will her weight and mass change on that planet? Explain.

____

____

____

____

Name ______________________

Date ______________________

Simple Machines

A. Explore Word Meanings

Think about the meaning of the words underlined below. Then use the definitions to place two simple machines from the box into each category.

A lever is a bar that pivots on a fixed point. An inclined plane is a slanted surface. A screw is a post with threads wrapped around it. A wedge is two inclined planes placed back to back. A pulley is made of a wheel with a line around it to change the direction of force. A wheel-and-axle is made of a wheel and an axle that turn together.

drill bit	**water faucet**	**axe**	**clothesline**
skateboard ramp	**wheelbarrow**	**cleaver**	**pry bar**
flag hoister	**salad spinner**	**nut and bolt**	**wheelchair ramp**

Lever	Inclined Plane	Screw
________	________	________
________	________	________

Wedge	Pulley	Wheel-and-axle
________	________	________
________	________	________

Name ______________________

Date ______________________

Lesson 1 - How Do Simple Machines Help People Do Work?

1. **Inquiry Skill Practice–Use Space Relationships**

Objects take up space and move through space in different ways. Scientists use these differences to make models. For example, how a rubber band stretches helps you "see" the force acting on it. How could you use space relationships to model Earth and its moon?

____

____

2. **Use Vocabulary**

Match the clue on the left to the term on the right.

____	The fixed point of a broom	**A.** simple machine
____	Has few or no moving parts	**B.** lever
____	The bar that pivots on a fixed point	**C.** fulcrum

3. 

Reading Skill Practice–Main Idea and Details

Read the selection. Underline the main idea. List at least 2 details.

Work is when force is used to move an object. The object must move in the direction of the force for work to be done. When you push a bicycle and it moves, you have done work. When you lift a box from the floor onto the table, you have also done work. But when you push a wall and it does not move, then work has not been done.

____

____

Name ______________________________

4. **Focus Skill** **Main Idea and Details**

Complete this graphic organizer. Give a definition and an example.

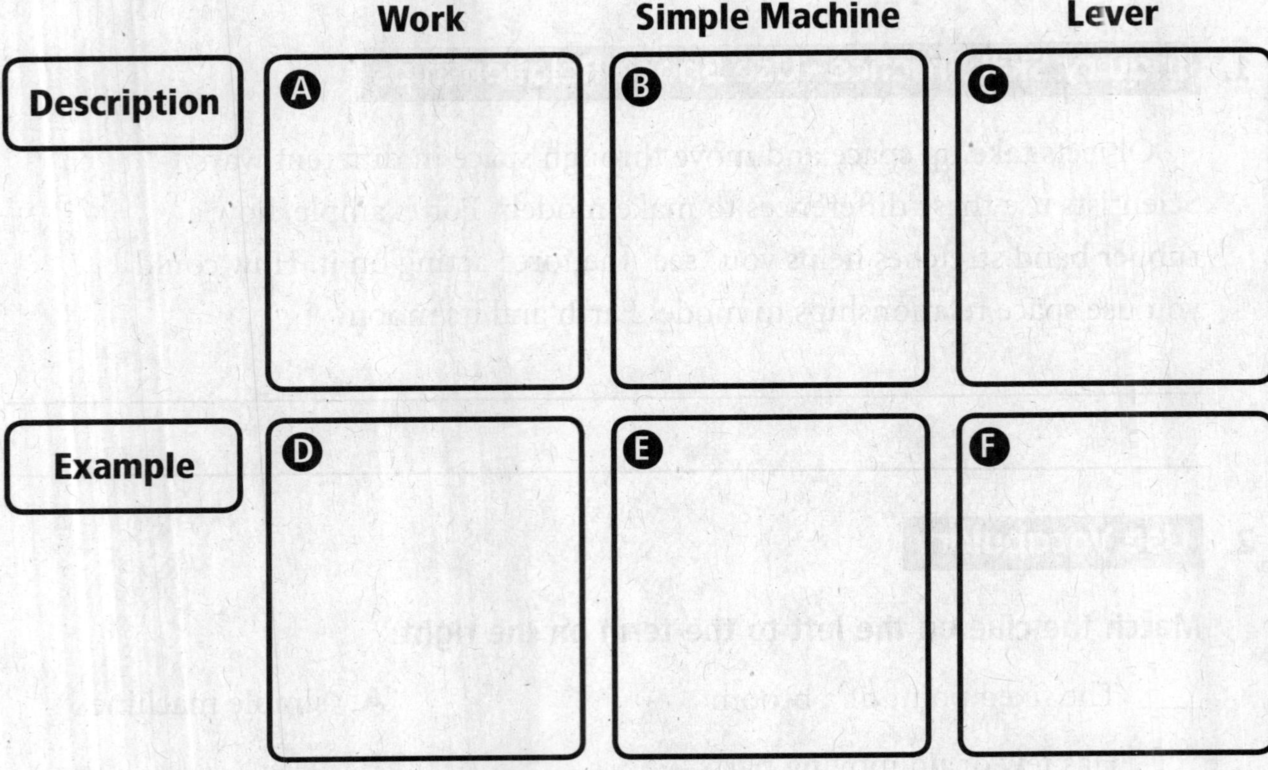

5. **Critical Thinking and Problem Solving**

Melissa uses a lever to move snow away from the driveway. What type of lever might she be using? How do you think she is using the lever? Explain using the word *fulcrum.*

____

____

____

____

Name ______________________________

Date ______________________________

Lesson 2 - How Do a Pulley and a Wheel-and-Axle Help People Do Work?

1. **Inquiry Skills Practice**

Suppose you are testing how pulley systems change the force you apply. Tell the variables you will control, change, and measure.

____

____

2. **Use Vocabulary**

Write a complete sentence that uses the term correctly.

pulley: ____

wheel-and-axle: ____

3. **Reading Skill Practice–Main Idea and Details**

Read the selection. Underline the main idea. List at least 2 details.

A pulley is a simple machine that makes work easier to do. A pulley is a wheel with a rope around it. When you pull the rope on the pulley one way, the other end of the rope goes the opposite way. When a bucket is dropped down in a well to take water out, a pulley is used. The rope is pulled down on one end, and the bucket comes up on the other. A single, nonmoving pulley does not change the force needed to lift the bucket.

____

____

Name ______________________________

4. **Main Idea and Details**

Complete this graphic organizer.

A pulley	A wheel-and-axle
is made up of	
Ⓐ ____________ ____________	Ⓒ ____________ that turns
with	
Ⓑ ____________ ____________	Ⓓ ____________ ____________

5. **Critical Thinking and Problem Solving**

Luis needs to lift a 50-pound box to a balcony on a second floor. The box is on a first floor. How many pounds will he be lifting if he uses a pulley to lift the box? Explain.

____

____

____

____

Name ______________________________

Date ______________________________

Lesson 3 - How Do Other Simple Machines Help People Do Work?

1. Inquiry Skill Practice–Interpret Data

Look at the data from a test of ramps. Do you think the data is reliable? Explain.

Trial	Ramp Length (cm)	Ramp Height (cm)	Force (N)
1	45	30	60
2	60	30	40
3	75	30	70
4	90	30	20

____

____

____

2. Use Vocabulary

Complete each sentence with the correct term from the box.

inclined plane screw wedge

A ________________ is a post with threads around it.

A sloped surface such as a ramp is called an

________________.

A ________________ is two inclined planes back to back.

3. Reading Skill Practice–Main Idea and Details

Read the selection. Underline the main idea. List at least three details.

Alex uses screws to make a bird house. He uses screws because they will hold the pieces of wood better than nails. Nails are smooth. They can slide out of the wood with time. Screws have threads wrapped

(cont'd.)

Name ___________________________

around them. The threads will help the screw stay in place. The screws will not slide out.

4. **Main Idea and Details**

Complete this graphic organizer by giving definitions and two examples of each machine.

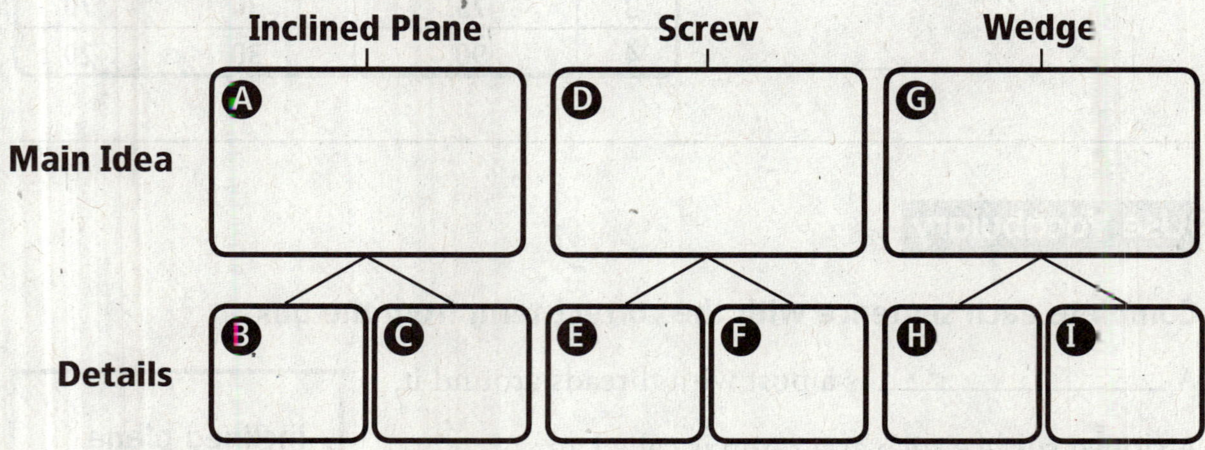

5. **Critical Thinking and Problem Solving**

Suppose you want to walk to the top of a steep hill. You can take the path that goes straight up, or you can take the path that winds around the hill. Use the words *force* and *distance* to explain what happens in each case.

VOCABULARY GAMES and CARDS

Contents

Note to Teachers: The vocabulary cards are listed in alphabetical order for each chapter. These cards are also provided in a different format in *Teaching Resources.* The two formats vary in order to assist with your photocopying needs.

Vocabulary Games

You can use the vocabulary cards on pages RS123–RS158 to play these games. The cards are provided for each chapter in your science textbook. Each card has a word on one side and the word's definition on the back. For some of these games, you may need to keep the definition hidden from view.

Guess the Word

You will need
vocabulary cards, paper and pencil

Grouping large groups or pairs

1. Form two teams. Each player must have a partner. One player in each pair is the clue giver, and one is the guesser.
2. Teams take turns playing. The first clue giver draws a word card and gives the guesser one clue at a time. Count clues to keep score.
3. After the word is guessed, play is passed to a pair on the other team. Use all the cards. The lowest score wins.

Word Ladder

You will need
vocabulary cards, tabletop

Grouping groups or partners

1. Place the cards in a pile, hiding the definitions.
2. Player 1 chooses a card, reads the word, and says the word's meaning. That player then turns the card over to check his or her answer.
3. If the meaning is correct, the word is placed near the edge of a tabletop. Player 1 continues until a word is missed. If more words are guessed correctly, the words are added to Player 1's ladder. If a word is missed, the card is returned to the pile. It is then the next player's turn.
4. The player who has formed the tallest ladder is the winner!

You will need

Hidden Words

vocabulary cards, paper and pencil

Grouping Whole class or large groups; small groups; pairs

1. Choose a word from the vocabulary cards to hide in a sentence. For example, the word *heat* is hidden in the following sentence: Mitch eats ice cream.
2. Write a sentence with a hidden word. Exchange papers with a classmate to find each other's hidden words.

You will need

Crossed Words

vocabulary cards, grid paper, and pencil

Grouping small groups or pairs

1. Place the cards face-up on a table so that each word can be seen. Choose one word for your crossword puzzle. Write that word vertically on the grid. Identify it by writing a number 1 in the box with the first letter, just as on a crossword puzzle. Use the word's definition on the back of the card to help write a clue for this starter word.
2. Choose a second word to add to the grid. Be sure it shares a letter with the first word written. Attach it to the first word by writing the second word horizontally on the grid. Identify it by writing a number 2 in the box with the first letter of that word.
3. Continue to attach words to the puzzle and number each word. Write clues for each of the numbered words.
4. Give a partner a blank grid with spaces numbered to match your puzzle. To help your partner solve the puzzle, shade each square of the grid that doesn't contain a letter. Challenge your partner to solve the puzzle by reading the clues and guessing each word.

Name That Word

You will need

2 identical sets of word cards; paper and pencil

Grouping small groups of at least five

1. One player is named as the "host." Players pair off into two teams. Each team has a set of word cards in the same order, placed facedown.
2. The host asks one person from each team to draw a card, checking to make sure both are looking at the same word. The player from Team A who saw the word goes first. He or she gives a one-word clue about the word. Team members then try to guess the word.
3. If the word is guessed, the host gives Team A a point. If the word is not guessed, Team B gets a turn. The player from Team B who saw the word gives a second one-word clue about the word. Team B then tries to guess the word. If the word is not guessed after five rounds, no team scores a point, and the host reveals the word to both teams.
4. After all of the cards have been drawn, the team with the most points wins.

Red Light, Green Light

You will need

vocabulary cards sorted by chapter, science textbook

Grouping large or small groups

1. Each player has a set of the same word cards. One person is the host of the game and does not play.
2. The host holds up one word for everyone to see. Each player then pulls that word card out of his or her pile. All players open their books to the chapter from which the word has been taken.
3. The host calls out "green light." Each player quickly looks for the word in a sentence. When a player finds the word, the word card marks the page and the book is closed. That player calls out "red light." Play then stops.
4. The player who stopped the game reads the sentence that holds the word. He or she scores one point. Play continues with the next word.

Wink, Wink

You will need
vocabulary cards, paper and pencil

Grouping groups or pairs

1. One player chooses a card and writes that word's definition. He or she then reads the word and says, "This word means..." The written definition is then read to the group. The player then winks at the group, reminding them that the definition may be correct, or it may have been invented.
2. Players take turns telling if they think the first player invented the definition, or if the correct meaning was given.
3. Any player guessing the correct response, earns a point. A second point is given to a player who can tell the correct definition when an invented definition was given.
4. Players take turns choosing word cards. The player with the most points at the end wins the game.

Word-O!

You will need
12 vocabulary cards for each player, 12 vocabulary cards for the caller, paper and pencil

Grouping large or small groups

1. Draw a tic-tac-toe board on your paper (two vertical lines crossed by two horizontal lines). Fill each space with a word from the word cards. Use a word only once.
2. A caller reads one word at a time. If one of your words is called, circle it.
3. When you have circled three words in a row, you have won! Call out, "Word-O!"

pan balance	**observation**
experiment	**scientific method**
hypothesis	**spring scale**
inference	**standard measure**
microscope	**bacteria**

Information from your senses.	A tool that measures mass.
A way scientists find out how things work and affect each other.	A test of a hypothesis.
A tool that measures forces, such as weight.	A statement of what you think will happen and why.
An accepted measurement.	An untested conclusion based on your observations.
Members of the kingdom of one-celled living things that lack nuclei.	A tool that makes an object look several times bigger than it is.

fungi	**protist**
invertebrates	**vascular**
microscopic	**vertebrates**
nonvascular	**direct development**
organism	**gene**

One of the kingdoms of living things that are one-celled.	Organisms that can't make food and can't move about.
Having tubes or channels.	The group of animals without backbones.
The group of animals with backbones.	Too small to be seen with the eyes alone.
A kind of growth in which an organism gets larger but doesn't go through other changes.	Without tubes or channels.
The basic unit of heredity.	A living thing.

heredity	**basic needs**
life cycle	**extinction**
metamorphosis	**fossil**
trait	**hibernation**
adaptation	**instinct**

Food, water, air, and shelter that an organism needs to survive.

The process by which traits are passed from parents to offspring.

The death of all the members of a certain group of organisms.

All the stages a living thing goes through.

The remains or traces of a plant or an animal that lived long ago.

Major changes in the body form of an animal during its life cycle.

A dormant, inactive state in which normal body activities slow.

A characteristic that makes one organism different from another.

A behavior that an animal begins life with.

A body part or behavior that helps an organism survive.

learned behavior	**diversity**
migration	**ecosystem**
abiotic	**environment**
biotic	**habitat restoration**
community	**pollution**

A great variety of living things.	A behavior that an organism doesn't begin life with.
A community and its physical environment together.	The movement of animals from one region to another and back.
All of the living and nonliving things surrounding an organism.	Describes a nonliving part of an ecosystem.
Returning a natural environment to its original condition.	Describes a living part of an ecosystem.
Waste products that damage an ecosystem.	All the populations of organisms living together in an environment.

population	**food chain**
carnivore	**food web**
consumer	**habitat**
decomposer	**herbivore**
energy pyramid	**niche**

A series of organisms that depend on one another for food.	All the individuals of the same kind living in the same ecosystem.
A group of food chains that overlap.	An animal that eats only other animals.
An environment that meets the needs of an organism.	A living thing that can't make its own food and must eat other living things.
An animal that eats only plants, or producers.	A living thing that feeds on the wastes and remains of plants and animals.
The role of an organism in its habitat.	A diagram showing how much energy is passed from one organism to the next in a food chain.

omnivore	clay
predator	erosion
prey	horizon
producer	humus
bedrock	igneous rock

The smallest particles that make up soil.	An animal that eats both plants and other animals.
The process of moving sediment from one place to another.	A consumer that eats prey.
A layer in the soil.	Consumers that are eaten by predators.
The remains of decayed plants or animals in the soil.	A living thing, such as a plant, that can make its own food.
A type of rock that forms from melted rock that cools and hardens.	The solid rock that forms Earth's surface.

metamorphic rock	**sedimentary rock**
mineral	**weathering**
rock	**deposition**
rock cycle	**earthquake**
sand	**fossil**

A type of rock that forms when layers of sediment are pressed together.	A type of rock that forms when heat or pressure change an existing rock.
The breaking down of rocks on Earth's surface into smaller pieces.	A solid nonliving substance that occurs naturally in rocks or in the ground.
The dropping of bits of rock and soil by a river as it flows.	A solid substance made up of one or more minerals.
The shaking of Earth's surface caused by movement of rock in the crust.	The sequence of processes that change rocks from one type to another over long periods.
The remains or traces of a plant or an animal that lived long ago.	The largest particles that make up soil.

fossil record	**volcano**
glacier	**air mass**
landform	**anemometer**
mountain	**barometer**
topography	**cold front**

A mountain that forms as lava flows through a crack onto Earth's surface.	The information about Earth's history that is contained in fossils.
A large body of air that has a similar temperature and moisture level.	A large, moving mass of ice.
A weather instrument that measures wind speed.	A natural feature on Earth's surface.
A weather instrument used to measure air pressure.	An area that is much higher than the land around it.
The boundary where a cold air mass moves under a warm air mass.	The shape of landforms in an area.

condensation	**precipitation**
evaporation	**rain**
hail	**rain shadow**
hurricane	**sea breeze**
land breeze	**sleet**

Water that falls to Earth.	The process by which a gas changes into a liquid.
Precipitation that is liquid water.	The process by which a liquid changes into a gas.
The area on the side of a mountain range that gets little rain or cloud cover.	Round pieces of ice formed when frozen rain is coated with water and refreezes.
A breeze that moves from the water to the land.	A large tropical storm that has winds of at least 74 miles per hour.
Precipitation made when rain falls through freezing-cold air and turns to ice.	A breeze that moves from the land to the water.

snow	**comet**
tornado	**constellation**
warm front	**galaxy**
water cycle	**moon**
axis	**moon phases**

A ball of rock, ice, and frozen gases in space.	Precipitation caused when water vapor turns directly into ice and forms ice crystals.
A pattern of stars that form an imaginary picture or design in the sky.	A fast-spinning spiral of wind that touches the ground.
A huge system of many stars, gas, and dust.	The boundary where a warm air mass moves under a cold air mass.
A natural body that revolves around a planet.	The movement of water from the surface of Earth into the air and back again.
The different shapes that Earth's moon seems to have.	The imaginary line around which Earth spins as it rotates.

orbit	**universe**
planet	**density**
solar system	**gas**
star	**liquid**
sun	**mass**

Everything that exists in space.	The path of one object in space around another object.
The amount of matter in an object compared to the space it takes up.	A large object that moves around a star.
The state of matter that does not have a definite shape or volume.	A group of objects in space that revolve around a central star.
The state of matter that has a definite volume but no definite shape.	A huge ball of superheated gases.
The amount of matter in an object.	The star at the center of our solar system.

matter	**state of matter**
mixture	**suspension**
solid	**volume**
solubility	**atom**
solution	**change of state**

One of the three forms (solid, liquid, and gas) that matter can exist in.	Anything that has mass and takes up space.
A kind of mixture in which particles of one ingredient are floating in another ingredient.	A blending of two types of matter that are not chemically combined.
The amount of space an object takes up.	The state of matter that has a definite shape and a definite volume.
The smallest unit of an element that has all the properties of that element.	The measure of how much of a material will dissolve in another material.
A physical change that occurs when matter changes from one state to another, such as from a liquid to a gas.	A mixture in which two or more substances are mixed completely.

chemical change	**matter**
chemical property	**physical change**
chemical reaction	**physical property**
compound	**absorption**
element	**amplitude**

Anything that has mass and takes up space.	A reaction or change in a substance, produced by chemical means, that results in a different substance.
A change in matter from one form to another that doesn't result in a different substance.	A property that involves how a substance interacts with other substances.
A trait that involves a substance by itself.	A chemical change.
The taking in of light or sound energy by an object.	A substance made of two or more different elements that have combined chemically.
A measure of the amount of energy in a wave.	A substance made up of only one kind of atom.

frequency	vibration
intensity	wavelength
pitch	conduction
reflection	convection
transmission	energy transfer

A quick back-and-forth motion.	A measure of the number of waves that pass in a second
The distance between a point on one wave and the identical point on the next wave.	A measure of how loud or soft a sound is.
The movement of heat between two materials that are touching.	A measure of how high or low a sound is.
The movement of heat in liquids and gases from a warmer area to a cooler area.	The bouncing of light, sound, or heat off an object.
A change of energy from one form to another.	The passing of light or sound waves through a material.

heat	waste heat
light	chemical energy
radiation	conductor
reflection	current electricity
refraction	electromagnet

Heat that can't be used to do useful work.	The flow of thermal energy from one object to another.
Energy that can be released by a chemical reaction.	A form of energy that can travel through space.
Materials that let electric charges travel through them easily.	The movement of heat without matter to carry it.
A steady movement of charges through certain materials.	The bouncing of light, sound, or heat off an object.
A temporary magnet caused by an electrical current.	The bending of light when it moves from one kind of matter to another.

generator	**magnet**
geothermal energy	**magnetic field**
hydroelectric power	**magnetic poles**
insulator	**mechanical energy**
kinetic energy	**electric motor**

An object that attracts iron and a few other (but not all) metals.	A device that makes an electric current.
The space around a magnet in which the force of the magnet acts.	Heat that comes from the inside of Earth.
The parts of a magnet at which its force is strongest.	Electrical energy made by using a dam and the kinetic energy of falling water.
The total potential and kinetic energy of an object.	A material that does not let current electricity move through it easily.
A device that changes electric energy to energy of motion.	The energy of motion.

parallel circuit	**acceleration**
potential energy	**force**
series circuit	**friction**
solar power	**gravitation**
static electricity	**gravity**

Any change in the speed or direction of an object's motion.	A circuit that has more than one path for an electric current to follow.
A pull or push of any kind.	Energy that an object has because of its position or its condition.
A force that resists motion between objects that are touching.	A circuit that has only one path for an electric current to follow.
A force that acts between any two objects and pulls them together.	The power of the sun.
The force of attraction between Earth and other objects, the expression of gravitation.	An electrical charge that builds up on an object.

inertia	**weight**
motion	**fulcrum**
position	**inclined plane**
speed	**lever**
velocity	**pulley**

A measure of the gravitational force acting on an object.	The property of matter that keeps an object at rest or keeps it moving in a straight line.
The fixed point on a lever.	A change of position of an object.
A simple machine that is a slanted surface	The location of an object.
A simple machine made of a bar that pivots on a fixed point.	The measure of an object's change in position during a unit of time.
A simple machine made of a wheel with a line around it.	The measure of the speed and direction of motion of an object.

screw	
simple machine	
wedge	
wheel-and-axle	
work	

	A simple machine made of a post with an inclined plane wrapped around it.
	A machine with few or no moving parts that you apply just one force to.
	A simple machine made of two inclined planes placed back to back.
	A simple machine made of a wheel and an axle that turn together
	The use of force to move an object over a distance.